Selected Longer Poems

Selected Longer Poems

....

A. R. AMMONS

W·W·NORTON & COMPANY

NEW YORK·LONDON

Copyright © 1980, 1975, 1972 by A. R. Ammons
Published simultaneously in Canada by George J. McLeod Limited,
Toronto. Printed in the United States of America.

First Edition

Library of Congress Cataloging in Publication Data

Ammons, A R   1926–
Selected longer poems.

I. Title.
PS3501.M6A6   1980   811'.5'4   79–17593
ISBN 0–393–01297–2
ISBN 0–393–00962–9 pbk.

1 2 3 4 5 6 7 8 9 0

with all my love to my son
John

Acknowledgments

A list of all my longer poems, arranged chronologically, would read as follows:

Tape for the Turn of the Year (published separately)
Pray Without Ceasing
Summer Session
Essay on Poetics
Extremes and Moderations
Hibernaculum
Sphere, the Form of a Motion (published separately)
Summer Place (*The Hudson Review*, Summer 1977)
The Snow Poems (published separately).

I am grateful to Jerald Bullis who suggested that a book such as this should be made available to go with *The Selected Poems 1951–1977* which contains shorter poems.

Contents

Pray Without Ceasing   1
Summer Session   16
Essay on Poetics   30
Extremes and Moderations   53
Hibernaculum   67

Selected Longer Poems

Pray Without Ceasing

I hear the low falling from the
highlands of hog-pasture, a music
of spheres, a couple: whatever is

done is to be
undone:
call me down from the
high places: I have achieved much
of the difficulty of my translation:

                     stock in trade
               gunstock
                     stockings
                     stocks & bonds & good
                     stock
          put no stock in that
                a stock case
             in stock
                     stock the soup

3, the mystical figure, comes through:
the alternating, suspended,
opposing spheres undirected and
the directed unity, reconciler and
putter to sleep—
milt on
the levees of rationality:

1

"O Aegypte,
Aegypte, of thy religious rites nought
will survive but tales
which thy children's children
will not believe;
nought
will survive but words graven upon
stones that tell of thy piety."
                         (Trismegistus)

and in sleep, as in a natural sleep,
prone, face turned as if into breath,
he had about him needments, bottles of
rare glass, bowls: we wrapped him
in reed mat, rose from decomposing,
generating waters, went up on
the plateau
and put him in
sand: hereafter has
not changed since for him:
but his head's
magnificence and funny-stuff, those
epicycles of motion, rituals of
turning, dancing, the wind
has taken, nothing
changed into grass: all the way
out of the rise and fall:

O Egypt I sometimes hear the
future of the universe
speaking in a moonwheel's
turning of sand and light:

we set out a withe of silver grass and
it remains: it
has interfered with the natural wind,
fractured the paralleleity of
moonbeams and disturbed
lesser sandstorms: mimicry
so often far more succeeds:

you heal back from napalm: the
flame-scars pull chin to chest,
the fingers stick: the mercy
of sand's
scarless:

when the sand roars, a lion
rouses in the center, his eyes,
as if in a hollow, headless:
recognition is
the fiercest imperative:

a pararox, couple achers: the
real estate of the imagination:

whatever is—
terror, pity, grief, death,
rising—a child sits in explosion's
clutter, homeless, his small
driftwood legs, his eyes inventing
an equal rage & dark, white smears
of burn
the mask
his face must fit:
whatever is, brutality, the inner siege,
the mind orange, blue with
desolation's mold, something
thin & high
cuts through whatever is
and makes no difference of difference:

my mouth, become eyes, weeps
words: words spill
into
hyacinths: for my acquaintance
with grief is
intimate, lost voices my credentials:
singing's been sung: the same
body is crying:

fatigues snagged by wire,

bodies sag in their buttons, collars
flutter, surf jogs, the wind
all outside and usual:
blue dusk fills up under the gold smoke:
the sky violates nothing to intercede:

I held her
by the rose and
intruded: the petals
slickened, silken: I shaved
my head &
offered it there:
O rose
the microflora along your hinder walls
are fast bloomers: tunnel-scapes
beady with stiff
moss: who keeps the saltsea keeps
its plankton, not reasonable?
microflora, reproducing, don't mind
the long glider that
coming shoulders out the wind to
fundamental suction: collapsible
I live with
spherical walls:
everyway I look leaning in, leaning in's
the style &
passing over: I pick pockets of
perse pansies, poesies, posepays,
powder palls & wary:

I had a little pony:
his name was Dapple Gray:
and every time I had him,
he tried to get away:

who will eat from such a garden
let him have an oedipal situation
and my rights and privileges:

that the triadic Hegel could have been

evidencing his
genitals is a notion of
such cracking solemnity
birds fail to fly:

some are spring harvests: today,
April Fools', a squirrel in the leafless
elm gathered torn bark and inner tissue
from dead branches, wadding them
into her mouth then going limb by
thinning limb to leap onto the heavy
electric wire, then going upstreet to my
neighbor's streetside spruce: I
think that's
where the nest will be:
waste assimilated into
use: the result a neatness
unpremeditated, a re-ingestion of
process:
so arranged it is that my wasted
life becomes words
that through complexity and
unstructured swirl
seek the fall-out of
comparable enhancements:

occurrences
    recognitions
        surroundings

                    tensions sprung free
                    into event

happenstance & necessity
    prediction & surprise
        moment & forever

and the gloomy, oh the melancholy,
remorseful
falling back and away

of time-sunk persons and places,
ragged knots
of a grounded, celestial kite:

yesterday robins
on the dark edge of dusk sang like
peepers:
I went out to listen
and they were robins:

and on the cold edge of spring
though on a warm day
we went out into the woods for
hepaticas up
along Six Mile Creek: we
found one spring-beauty and
by sun-warmed logs
a few clusters of hepatica,
hundreds of plants
but few bloomers: the
backfall of creekwater was
interesting, countercaps, and
compensating, the up-creek water
along eddying banks:

peripheries:
the dance about the fire,
utterance of tongues,
parlance of feet:
griefs can't be removed,
only altered, caught up into the
timed motions
of bearable sway:

fall in love with yourself
where it's shallow:
don't
thwart shriveling up by
suddenly drowning:

if change is certain, as say so many,
certainty is where there isn't any:

> pop gun
> soda pop
> pop art
> popsicle
> mom & pop
> popinjay
> pop in
> popeyed
> population

I can't get that star carted I said:
flooded carburetor, cracked voltage
regulator: I didn't realize at once
it was apt: a Starchief: and
one day a man said looking at
the dash word, it has
your name in it: St*archie*f: he
was a good abstractor:

I had a little pony:
his name was Dapple Gray:
and when I tried to trim him,
he had a lot to bray:

an inch of snow last night but
mid morning is bright and melting:
the shadows are white:

napalm isn't falling here:
so what is it:

first, an explosion near the ground:
then a tarry rain,
soft and afire, falls, crumbles, & sticks:
sticks to trees, houses, children,
things like that: if
it hits it's 94.3% effective:

I see my death, my horror, the radical,
real, senseless pain,
as a coming afloat,
rocking in a mastery of oceans:
what time caricatures should
time keep:
to those busy making themselves
great, with grave music and
solemn looks, a thorough using up and
setting forth of language's materials,
I send
empty statements, slip-shoddiness,
incredible breeziness and such:
the wind we go to
understands everything:
I sing, though, in a way, the best I can,
for I may be understood
where I do not understand:

around the aureola matters get touchy:

confusion erodes the ice-glass
steel offices buildings of rationality:
anti-rationality only makes another
kind of thrust: complexity
blurs the sleek towers, wilts the
phallus of mistaken direction:

welcome to your unattended,
coin-operated, do-it-yourself
laundry:
bring and use your favorite bleach,
soap, and starch: if
machine is
defective, please use another machine:
to start washer put money in coin meter
and
(1) if slide type meter—slowly push
slide all the way in: then slowly
pull slide all the way out:

(2) if rotary knob type meter—
turn knob:
tub
will start filling not later than ½
minute after operating coin slide:

> stopcock
> > cock & bull
> ears cocked
> > cocktail
> peacock
> > cockle
> > cockney
> > cockiness
> > cockscomb
> poppycock
> > cockeyed
> > cockroach
> > cockpit
> > cocksure

dryclean wash 'n wears, even cotton
items: use this
handy clothing guide: follow
these simple steps:
brush away loose lint
and other soiling matter: turn sweaters
inside out: turn down cuffs of
trousers: insert the
necessary coins:

rubbers, after several drycleanings,
tend to lose elasticity: plastic-coated
fabrics often become stiff.
beware sequins, beads, and other fragile
ornaments, can get you into trouble:

remove wear wrinkles and sharpen creases

and pleats: some spots refuse
to come out, rust, mildew, dried paint,
indelible ink:

little artery, couple inches long,
branching into cardiac muscle: it pops
and you give up philosophy and
ultimate concern, car payments, son and wife,
you give up the majors & minors,
the way you like your egg cooked, your
class ring, lawn,
sparrows nesting in the garage, the
four crocus bulbs (maybe more next
year), toenails and fillings:

I wouldn't want to happen up on any
critters of eternity, absolutes that
end the world: fellow said one star
up there in our galaxy is mostly
gadolinium, a rare earth;
nobody knows how the concentration occurred:
then there are other surpluses and
scarcities
that uneven the tissue:
I wouldn't want anything
to get known tight: ignorance is our
boat giving us motion: or, capsized,
knowledge is our ark which is more in
line with the tradition:
        the ocean would then
        be what it
        is:

spirit, though
it encompasseth mightiness, etc., however,
cannot, like a motor,
raise and lower
toast:

nothing matters, believe me, except

everything: to sift & sort, magnify
& diminish, admit & renounce, impairs
the event:
what the mind can't accept's obscene:
the rest shines with an
additional, redeeming
light,
the light in the head
of language in motion:

the wave coming in, running, gathers,
lofts, curls—the instant of
motion's maximum
organization: then: then one is
forty & hollow: the curl's reach
redeems the hollow, equals it, till
the curl touches over: what is the
use: the crashing, the hollow coming
topside into wide prevalence,
the flat waters skinnying out and
rushing back—is merely endurance
until the next wave lifts:
as for what's left,
dip it and ship it: to have made
it here is not to have it made:

entering is lovely:
such delicacies, scents, the
feminine source, perfumes: cookies
in the oven, delights:

mixmaster, mixmaster,
mast me a mix, ur,
mix me a mist, ur . . .
the mixers and blenders chew up
differences: chomp & whirl
to knotless paste: the spurt for
equilibrium:
to compensate for which somewhere root,
bark, leaf must make a walnut, some

skinny saint rail through the cosmos,
shot from earth by penury and dread:
what is more costly or
needed than a mind shot to space by
shiny thrust, a renunciation of
earth, a negative blast away:

I have seen all the way in with
a white bang that they
are spheres, round solids, sprinkled,
lightly, in a medium, not
empty, called space and that
these round bodies go round
different orders of center
that swoosh away burning
their peripheries and sucking
their centers through virgin space, neither
up nor
down—the
terror that that is
the way it is,
that particular way, a
pure flower of terror:

ancient souls sitting on
the bright banks of forever
in
raptures of old acquaintance: for every
never again,
an always again: and young souls
from their quick missing
quick as branches and glittering:
where the lost remains, immortal in
the foreverness of the lost:
say good morning, say buon giorno,
say hi
to infant brother, to mother, father,
sit down under the golden pines on
the slopes of no further parting:

the Buddhist nun burns for the peace
her ashes will achieve:

the village woman coming home finds
her shack afire, her
son & husband shot: she bends down
where she is:
she is given tokens of the dead but
her left arm like a sickle reaps at the
air
for the harvest
already taken:

through the reeds somewhere, as by a
paddy or ditch in her head,
wind burrs
a leaf: the woman flutters,
her grief absolute and
not a mystery:

how can I know I
am not
trying to know my way into feeling
as

feeling
tries to feel its way into knowing:
it's
indifferent what I say: the motions
by which
I move
manifest
merely a deeper congruence
where the structures are:

run my poem through your life and
exist, decommissioned,
like rubble,
innocent, slouchy on the uptake:

the scramblers, grabbers, builders—
rubblerousers: sticking stone to
false stone in a unity of walls which
wants to come apart: let
weeds and grasses move in among a
scattering, make a little shade, hide
mice, give burrows to ground bees,
byway hideouts to the engines of spiders,
stones the
owl can come and sit in moonlight on:
we
should all be in a shambles, shacked up,
peeping round the grasshoppers,
preserving a respectful quiet:

don't snatch & grab: grab snatch:
laboratory tests attest,
when a system of two bodies
charges and discharges itself
it's peaceful as tulips:

can a 41-year-old man living on dandelion leaves
from the cool edges of junkyards
find
songlore enough
in the holocausts, boggy garbage,
fly swarms, lamb bones, and rust-floral
cans
of his weedy search
to sustain interest:

the continuum, one
and visionless, within
which
the breakdown of pure forms,
arising of skyscrapers, laws,
the high crystal-clear arising
of theory:

the evening blue-purple, the trees
black,

the birds can't quit singing: damp
heat built
and rose through the golden towered afternoon,

broke finally into motion, as of
descent, rain beating
straight down
between racks of thunder:

can anything be erased: can this day's
praising hold to the day it praises
down the slopes of total entropy:

pray without ceasing:

we found hailstones in the grass
and ate them to cool:
spurred stones
with interior milkwhite halos,
an arrested spangling:
the high hard water
melted
aching our tongues.

Summer Session

Saliences are humming bee paths
in & out around
here, continuous if
unpredictable: they
hang the air with cotton
candy
and make a neighborhood:

we set out four tomato plants a while
ago: good soil
where a row of winter-used cut wood was
I've been out several times to see
but coming dark hinders me,
forcing faith up which
must
spindly as high walloping
weeds
outlast the night:

earlier came a shower so
skinny
not a coil spring in the glass pond
rang the periphery, for a minute:

walking home from class:
dogs yurping
out from hedge tunnels,
jerking to snazzy, skidding halts,

an outrage about the legs,
hairy explosion with
central, floating teeth:
I hope snitching hairy little
worms
will thread their eyelids and distending close off
the eyeballs of flagrant sight the way
summer closed up the
hedges to fill
us with surprises:

in my yard's more wordage than I
can read:
the jaybird gives a shit:
the earthworm hoe-split bleeds
against a damp black clump:

the problem is
how
to keep shape and flow:

the day's died
& can't be re-made:
in the dusk I can't recover
the goldenbodied fly
that waited on a sunfield leaf:

well I can't recover the light:
in my head—on the
inside frontal wall—the fly waits
and then, as he did, darts upward at an
air-hung companion:

ghosts remain, essences out-skinnying
light: essences
perceiving ghosts skinny skinny
percipients:
reverence, which one cannot
withhold, is

laid on lightly, with terror—as if
one were holding a dandelion back
into the sun:

all these shapes my bones
answer to
are going to go on
consuming, the flowers, venations, vines,
the roots that know their
way,
going to go on taking down and
re-designing, are going to go on
stridently
with bunchers & shears
devouring sundry mud, flesh: but their
own shapes will, as will all shapes, break
but will with all
others
cast design ahead where possible, hold
figuration in the cast seed:
shape & flow:
we must not feel hostile:

the most perfect nothingness affords
the widest play,
the most perfect meaninglessness:
look up at dusk and see
the bead fuzzy-buzzy bug
no darker than mist:
couldn't get along
at all except against infinity:
swallow, bat dine
in a rush—
never know what hit him
nothing hit him sent him to nothing:
but the temporary marvels!—
getting along against. . . .
take it from there:

(to slink and dream with the interior singing
attention of snakes)

prolix as a dream, a stream, sameness
of going
but diverse, colorful, sunlit
glints and glimmerings:
can motion alone then
hold you, strange person:
entertainments of flame and water,
flame in water,
an honorable, ancient flame
removed in high burning: water
no less a metal of interest, subtly
obeying: sit down and be consoled:
the death that reaches toward you has
been spared none:
be enchanted with the shrill hunger
of distant children:
do something:

the boughs ripen:
birds falling out
around here like plums,
rolling around, tilting over, turbulent
somersaults, a wrestling with divinity,
smooth & mostly belly:
the tail's a mean instrument but
feathered
gives poise, as of
contrary knowledges:
the cats frizzling with interest tone
down to pure motion: songs go
such way:
destruction of the world into the
guts: regeneration:
the kill is a restless
matter: but
afterwards the fact's
cool as satiation:

we just had lunch at the picnic table
under the elm: chunks of cantaloupe,
peach slices, blueberries, all cool
colorings in a glass cup: hotdogs &
pepsi:
brilliant replenishment:
icy destructions with the berry
burst, the teeth in a freshet
of cantaloupe juice:
the robin's nest, way out on a pear
limb, nearly
overhangs the table: some
worry, of course, a chirp or two:
distant approaches: above, the yellow
triangles of mouths:

up the stairs you go
up the stairs you go
beddybye &
snoozy snooze
up the stairs you go
ho ho
up the stairs you go

now the lawnmowers of reality are
whirring on the slopes of absent lawns
and sunday is in the world or part
of it: I look across the valley
to the otherside big hills and realize
the whole thing's rolling
tumbling in the smoothest quietest
lunge, our
bristlegreen rockship, our clamorous
house wherein difference bites so
hard hardly
a man will admit the common nickelodean core
where metals twist in
slow drifts of warping
pressure:

nevertheless into raw
space we turn, sun
feeding cosmic drift through,
expelling radiance of cosmic storm,
and we are at an
incredible height going round
something:
in the whole coming and going of man
we may not
get around once:
at certain levels recurrence is not
a bore: we clip an arc:

buttered batter's better bitter:

what do you know:
Western Prong beat Old Dock:
stir up them little wasps and you
have a nest of hornets:

past 2 1
women suffer
unbearably (!)
take bladder irritation: that headachy
backachy feeling:
that burning stitching itching gives them
the weewee's, makes them need
fast relaxing comfort: what women go
through
to make or lose a buck: in those
ample haunches
greased with sheer illumination's light
is a mess of bacterial bloomers: it's
merciful to lust the eye's
small-blind: cultures from average nipples:
knowledge is lovely
but some of it shivers
into the blood stream
and undermines the

requirements of the moment: but
desire spills antiseptic gold celluloid
sheathes o'erall
and pours pellucid lubricants
down the drains of microfloral
habitations:
the clitoris rises above
surmountings, backs off, and
takes a testy peck or so:

we went to the park & John swung on
the swings and swung:
little children, I told my wife,
these little children, some of them
will live to say two thousand forty
maybe forty-five, fifty:
I said think of it by that time
we, you and I, will have been dead
so long
worms yet will scoff at us:
it makes you think
(twice):
what are
a few vaginal weeds in the teeth
compared with the traipsing gluebellies of
candorous maggots: & other worms,
all their noise:
get down, yes:
enwarm to eradication the carnal
longings: which are short:

what, then, is the organization of the
soul: scrambles to the peak,
squirts off, slumps back: the
long & short of it:

ducks were there, spinning, sputtering
in the glass: popcorn, wiener rolls
floating in the circumstance: but do
they do do underwater:

if a scientist, I'd devise
a test
and count the dropping abstractions off:
a glass tank with top
and a careful observer
could keep that duck in there
till he had to: yes, but the
test's wrong: suppose the observed's
disturbed & would much have
preferred
to go out upon the ground & hunker up on
a hunk of grass:
could turn to billets due
formerly:
following a duck around au naturel
though
could wobble a man's weltanschauung:
scientific objectivity puts
radiance on
duckshit even: we used to save
coop chickenshit for choicest
garden plants:
a powerful ingredient that
through the delicacies of floral
transfiguration
makes tasty gravy:

friend of mine, brilliant
linguist, told me
a Southern Gentleman screwed
himself in the
penis
with a squirrel's
pizzle:
puzzling:
got it hung in there's how everybody
found out:
doctor had to cut it loose:

let approved channels then be your

contemplation
so you will not wind up in a fix
or fuxy fox, feel the fire asphaltic:
do
not go in for strange devices:
pins, strangulations or such:
practices that lead gradually away
from picnic tables,
the trivial fluvial fumes of sunday braziers:

I'm not going to
delay my emergence:
I'm going to plop
a polyp:
I'm going to pupate
pussycoon:
I'm going to shoot for the wings:
I can't tell you how many times with
stalled interior I've
watched the spiders hatch & thrive:
I'm going to
get something off my chest—
incubus or poking heartflipper:
I'm 42:
the rank & file has
o'errucked me & cloddled on:
I'm not going
any longer officially
to delay my emergence:
I want the head of the matter to
move out of skinny closure:
I want a pumping, palpable turgidity:
I want the condition to take on flare:
I want manifestation silk-dry:

I told this fellow:
I met him out under a soaking
elm tree:
I said you're needy:

you're so needy something's rotten:
I told him just because you have a
mailbox doesn't mean anybody has
to put anything in it:
it's your epidermal hole, nobody else's:
I was getting so much pleasure out
of soaking under the elm tree I
couldn't get interested in the guy's nasty cavity
and knew without looking I wasn't
going to put anything in there:
too bad about the elms being in dutch:

Archie:
    Summer Session has agreed (somewhat
reluctantly) to split 303 into 2
sections, with one for Baxter. I
haven't been able to reconfirm with Bax
that he does still want a second course
but I've gone ahead as if he did, with
the understanding that *someone* will
teach the plus-23 students and do so
at the same time (8:00) as you.
                    Barry

seeing in a green yard a sailboat for sale:
worth a morning:
when you consider life
adds up
to exactly nothing:

one day I'm
going to go
out & conjure
the clouds down:
I'm going to try the cape on:
if they don't
come right down
flubbing their responsive damp bellies over the
ambience

I'm going to strip and shit:

as a writing teacher I tell them
revise the world:
they clip, trim, slice:
they bring it in:
oh no I say you've just put it on
stilts:
they lob, twist, crack:
oh no I say when they bring it in
you've killed it:
reconceive:
they bring in something new:
what's the use, I throw up my hands,
we're already two or three worlds
behind:

down this drain, endless
ingestion, getting
bloated with world: anybody toss
an old memo in: it's squirting
milk into treeping squabs:
burning's going on down
there:
the whole world's a few flakes:
it's sedimentation through seas:
those in the heights need
substantial bottoms: need the
sense
things are leveling off: hate
wide, especially open, disparities:

equilibrium fills holes with hills:

feed in a grocery list, somebody:
feed in how to fix a
telescope on, say, a comet: feed in a
few large pieces of legislation,
couple committee reports, some lab

notes, triptickets, sailing schedules,
the dawns & dusks of planets,
contemplations of squirrels:

somewhere along the line the computer
is going to perpetrate a large announcement:
then we'll know why the
imagination's
winding no scraps up into
windy transfigurations:
in our day
comfort is sunrise at 5:25:

couple systems analysts: bushel of
female ticks, engorged: some dirty
rats:
cutworms:
nightfeeders that dusk arouses:
cubic mile of infestation,
corruption, rust, pus, pus
caterpillars,
snot:
tank of wound weepage:
boxcar of love salt,
fill, siftings, winnowings, dregs,
curds, chips,
aerosols of eagerness, dozen black
widows:
a league of universal ivy stone:
choice:
much testament of need: 400
singing horses, a flask of
wart-juice from the udders of the awry:

families with a lot of living to do:
should get turquoise, shaded coppertone,
or spanish avocado:

features for fun-loving families:

discover for yourselves where
the problems are & amass
alternative strategies:
otherwise it's D–& no pussy:

Archie:
     Thanks very
much. That's a
real pleasure.
                        Neil

I scribble, baby, I mean
I breeze on:
every mile a twist, I
should be back:
a smidgen slit of silence lets all
in:
the land's turning tables
greased with the finest silence
money can buy, still, the wind, mine & its,
rattles over the ridges, splits
the cords of wood & gristle:
to a cartographer
part of Pennsylvania's a broken record:
curving grooves & ridges in
visual music:

day after day the camels of the rain
bear their gray way by: the ditches
bend green grass in:
but then drought enlarges in rapids
the incidence of rocks:
but then flood, so salient, though
with muscle swirls, could
scrape you across a single
prominence,
splitting possibility like a paper shell:
it is, even after an 8-day rain,

hard to know what to ask for:
a baby robin's been out on the
lawn all day, all day wet and for
many days wet though only one
day out: maybe if it were
dry he could get to a low branch at
least, some force from those fumbling
wings, airier dry:

here are the 18-year-old
seedbeds & the
19-year-old fertilizers:
they have come for a summer session:
knowledge is to be my insemination:
I grant it them as one grants flesh
the large white needle:
what shall I tell those who are
nervous,
too tender for needles, the
splitting of iridescent tendons:
oh I tell them nothing can realize
them, nothing ruin them
like the poundage of pure self:
with my trivia
I'll dispense dignity, a sense of office,
formality they can define themselves against:
the head is my sphere:
I'll look significant as I deal with
mere wires of light, ghosts of
cells, working there.

Essay on Poetics

Take in a lyric information
totally processed, interpenetrated into
wholeness where

a bit is a bit, a string a string, a
cluster a cluster, everything beefing up
and verging out

for that point in the periphery where
salience bends into curve
and all saliences bend to the same angle of

curve and curve becomes curve, one curve, the whole curve:
that is information actual
at every point

but taking on itself at every point
the emanation of curvature, of meaning, all
the way into the high

recognition of wholeness, that synthesis,
feeling, aroused, controlled, and released:
but then find the wholeness

unbelievable because it permits
another wholeness,
another lyric, the same in structure,

in mechanism of existence, but bearing a different weight,

that is, a different, perhaps contradicting,
bit-nature and assimilation:

wholeness then is a condition of existence,
a one:many mechanism, internally irrelevant to scope,
but from the outside circumscribed into scope:

I like the order that allows, say, when
a thousand cows are on a thousand acres,
clusters to flow out in single file down a gully,

encirclings of drinkholes, concentrations in a green
bottom, spread-outs, but identifiable, across
a broad rise or scape: I like that just as I

like tracings converging into major paths,
untracings of widening out beyond a clump of
trees or small pass:

those configurations, rendered by aerial photography,
would interest me endlessly
in the precision of their topographical relations:

the interests of cows and the possibilities of
the landscape could be read (not a single actual cow)
there well: and nothing be as a consequence known and

yet everything in a sense known, the widest paths
the controlling symbols, with lesser resemblances of
motion: after a while I could account for the motions of

the whole herd and make interesting statements:
for example, with experience, I bet I could tell
from the wear under a copse

whether a lot of hot sunny days in a year
or windy days come: I could tell something obvious already
from the copse whether it constitutes a meaningful

windbreak in a cold wind, sand or snow storm, and then
that, though obvious, would tell about cows:

I'll bet in warm climates with heavy, maybe daily, rains

there'd be little wear under trees, for the cows
would enjoy being out in the showers:
anyway, there's a time when loose speech has to give in,

come up to the corral, run through the planked alleys,
accept the brand, the medication, surrender to the
identity of age, sex, weight, and bear its relationship

to the market: there's no market for most speech, specially
good, and none for loose: that's why I don't care
how far I wander off;

I wouldn't care if I found a whole year gone by and myself
not called for: the way I think is
I think what I see: the designs are there: I use

words to draw them out—also because I can't
draw at all: I don't think: I see: and I see
the motions of cowpaths

over a non-existent, thousand-acre ranch: (times
frequently recur in good scope in which I don't see):
stop on any word and language gives way:

the blades of reason, unlightened by motion, sink in,
melting through, and reality's cold murky waters
accept the failure: for language heightens by dismissing reality,

the sheet of ice a salience controlling, like a symbol,
level of abstraction, that has a hold on reality and suppresses
it, though formed from it and supported by it:

motion and artificiality (the impositional remove from reality)
sustain language: nevertheless, language must
not violate the bit, event, percept,

fact—the concrete—otherwise the separation that means
the death of language shows: when that happens abandonment
is the only terrible health and a return to bits, re-trials

of lofty configurations: if the organism of the ranch
alters, weeds will grow in old paths and the new waterhole
exist in a new weaving: means, reaching identity too

soon, exclude: mannerism is more suitable to the lyric
than to larger affairs because both lyric and manneristic style
are slight completions: dropping back from the completion

to a linear mode can be more engrossing: for example, the
dactyllic hexameter can grind on, entangling, ingesting bits,
threads, strings, lesser saliences into considerable scope: or

iambic pentameter, especially unrhymed, is an infinitely various
ployable means: one must be ever in search of the rapier that
holds the world on guard: but the sparrow trap traps a sparrow:

(disquisition is sesquipedalian pedestrianism, tidying up
the loose bits, but altogether missing the import of the impetus):
a center's absolute, if relative: but every point in spacetimematter's

a center: reality is abob with centers: indeed, there is
nothing but centers: centers of galaxies, systems, planets, asteroids,
moons, drifts, atoms, electrons: and the center, as of the

earth, where all turns and pressures meet, is inexpressibly light,
still, and empty: the spruce trees at this moment deeply
sway with snow and snow is falling, the temperature below

freezing: the muffled morning offered no relief: now, though;
just after noon, small gusts twist the branches: not
the heavy lower branches, too long in their holding, and too wide,

to respond: but twist the lighter, higher branches so they drop
falls of snow and those falls, light, their efficacy increased
by falling, strike the lower, heavier loads, dislodging airy

avalanches, sketchy with event but releasing: it seems to me
a possibility of unceasing magnitude that these structures
permit these eventualities: small winds with small branches can

loosen heavy postures: a miraculous increase, as if heat could
go uphill: but occurring within a larger frame, at great potential
expense: (but energy displacements, switches, translations are

too considerable for calculation in the smallest sector): still,
though the whole may be running down, spills
here and there are overspills, radiances: the lyric, then,

has never been found out because at the center it, too, is
empty, still, silent: this is a point of provisional
summation: hence, the *then's*, *still's*, and *but's:*

a point of entangling toward the intertwining of a core, a core
involving every thread: so far, we have ranch, snowsquall,
avalanche, ice skates, wind, etc.: but the main confluence

is one:many which all this essay is about: I get lost for fun,
because there's no chance of getting lost: I am seeking the
mechanisms physical, physiological, epistemological, electrical,

chemical, esthetic, social, religious by which many, kept
discrete as many, expresses itself into the
manageable rafters of salience, lofts to comprehension, breaks

out in hard, highly informed suasions, the "gathering
in the sky" so to speak, the trove of mind, tested
experience, the only place there is to stay, where the saints

are known to share accord and wine, and magical humor floats
upon the ambient sorrow: much is nearly stable there,
residencies perpetual, more than less, where gold is utterly

superfluous and paves the superfluous streets, where phenomena
lose their drift to the honey of eternity: the holy bundle of
the elements of civilization, the Sumerians said: the place

where change is mere disguise, where whatever turns turns
in itself: there is no reason for confusion: that is
what this is about: it's simple and impossibly difficult,

simple by grandeur, impossible by what all must answer there:
enterprise is our American motif, riding horseback between
the obscure beginning and the unformulated conclusion, thinking

grace that show of riding, the expertise, performance, the intricacy
of dealing: to be about something: history can assign and glean,
furnish sources and ends, give grades: that is the

enterprise of history, always best when best accomplished: since
the one thing we learn from history is that we do not learn:
enterprise then's the American salience, rainbow arch,

colossus: but the aristoi are beauty, wealth, birth, genius &
virtue who should be gouvernors: enterprise somewhat, though
not necessarily, inconsistent with those, we lack governors:

the definition of definition goes two ways, opposing:
one direction cuts away, eliminating from relevance, limits
into true: take the word *true:* it goes back through ME.

treue, trewe to AS. *treowe, trywe* to a kinship with G. *treu*
and on to IE. *derew,* meaning tree, in the basic sense of as
firm as a tree: if one could be sure of Indo-European forests

one might add lofty, abundant, straight, strong, majestic:
somewhere then in the essence of *tree* has been found the
essence of *true*, including perhaps the perpendicularity or

verticality of true: but while *tree* clarifies the
mind with certain boundaries, it also recalls clusters
of tree-images, memories of particular

simple by grandeur, impossible by what all must answer there:
enterprise is our American motif, riding horseback between
the obscure beginning and the unformulated conclusion, thinking

then to turn the essential image of a tree into the truest
rational wordage: truth, then, might be "conformity
with the facts": but then we know that facts have truth

when touched, given configuration by transforming,
informing fiction: is this unnecessarily
puzzling: all I mean to suggest is that the reality under

words (and images) is too multiple for rational assessment and
that language moves by sailing over: the
other way definition has is to accept the multiplicity of

synthesis: of course, synthesis is at work in certain levels of
analysis, but I mean by synthesis the primary intent: look
at it this way: I am experiencing at the moment several

clusters of entanglement: if I took a single thread from a
single cluster, viewed it, explained it, presented it, would
I not be violating my reality into artificial clarity and my

bundles into artificial linearity: but if I broached, as I seem
to be doing, too many clusters, would I not be violating this
typewriter's mode into nonsense: hue a middle way, the voice

replied, which is what I'm doing the best I can,
that is to say, with too many linking verbs: the grandest
clustering of aggregates permits the finest definition: so out

of that bind, I proceed a little way into similarity and
withdraw a bit into differentiae: unfortunately, man cannot
do better though it might be better done: if I begin with

the picture of a lyre, translate it into a thousand words,
do I have a lyric: what is a lyre-piece: a brief and single
cry: the quickest means to a still point in motion:

three quatrains rhyming alternate lines: let me see if I can
write a poem to help heave the point:

At Once

Plumage resembles foliage
for camouflage often

and so well at times it's difficult

to know whether nature means
resembler or resembled:
obviously among things is

included the preservation of
distinction in a seeming oneness:
I say it not just

because I often have: maximum
diversity with maximum unity
prevents hollow easiness.

                                        poetry, even in its
self-rationale aims two ways at once, polar ways sometimes

to heighten the crisis and pleasure of the reconciliation:
getting back to *tree* and *true*, though, I was thinking last
June, so multiple and dense is the reality of a tree, that I

ought to do a booklength piece on the elm in the backyard here:
I wish I had done it now because it could stand for truth, too:
I did do a sketch one day which might suggest the point:

I guess it's a bit airy to get mixed up with
an elm tree on anything
like a permanent basis: but I've had it
          worse before—talking stones and bushes—and may
          get it worse again: but in this one
the elm doesn't talk: it's just an object, albeit
    hard to fix:
unfixed, constantly
influenced and influencing, still it hardens and enters
the ground at a fairly reliable point:
especially since it's its
general unalterability that I need to define and stress
          I ought to know its longitude and latitude,

so I could keep checking them out: after all, the ground
drifts:
and rises: and maybe rises slanting—that would be
difficult to keep track of, the angle
          could be progressive or swaying or
seasonal, underground rain
& "floating" a factor: in hilly country
                the underground mantle, the
"float" bedrock is in, may be highly variable and variable
in effect:
I ought to know the altitude, then, from some fixed point:
I assume the fixed point would have to be
   the core center of the planet, though I'm perfectly
prepared to admit the core's involved
      in a slow—perhaps universal—slosh that would alter the
      center's position
      in terms of some other set of references I do not
      think I will at the moment entertain
      since to do so invites an outward, expanding
      reticulation
      too much to deal precisely with:

      true, I really ought to know where the tree is: but I know
      it's in my backyard:
      I've never found it anywhere else and am willing to accept
                the precision of broadness: with over-precision
      things tend to fade: but since I do need stability and want
      to make the tree stand for that (among other things)
      it seems to me I ought to be willing to learn enough about
      theory and instrument
      to take sights for a few days or weeks and see if anything
      roundly agreeable could be winnowed out: that
      ought to include altimeters (several of them, to average
      instrumental variation), core theory and gravity waves:
      but I'm convinced I'm too awkward
      and too set in some ways
      to take all that on: if I am to celebrate multiplicity,
      unity, and such
      I'll be obliged to free myself by accepting certain
      limitations:

                    I am just going to take it for granted
                    that the tree is in the backyard:
              it's necessary to be quiet in the hands of the marvelous:

I am impressed with the gradualism of sway,
of growth's sway: the bottom limb that John's
swing's on and that's largely horizontal
has gradually outward toward the tip
      demonstrated the widening of the leaves
by
sinking: the rate of sinking, which is the rate of
growth, has been
within the variations of night and day, rain and shine,
broadly constant
and the branch's adjustment to that growth
      of a similar order: nevertheless, the
wind has lifted, a respiratory floating, the branch
as if all the leaves had breathed in, many a
time
and let it fall
and rain and dew have often lowered it below its depth—
birds have lighted bringing
varying degrees of alteration to the figurings, sharp
distortions, for example, to the
twigs, slow dips to secondary branches, perhaps no
noticeable effect at the branch root:
              I should go out and measure the diameters of
the branch, secondary branches, small limbs, and twigs
and their extensions from base
and devise a mathematics
to predict the changes of located average birds: it
would give me plenty to do for weeks
and save me from the rigors of many heights:
or scoot me to them: conceiving a fact stalls the
imagination to its most threatening dimension:

I think now of growth at the edges of the leaves as the
reverse of the elmworm's forage:

the elmworm, I haven't seen any this year—one spring

there were millions—is as to weight an interesting
speculation:
as he eats the leaf lessens but of course the weight is
added to himself, so on a quick scale the
transformation is one to one:
but the worm makes waste, the efficiency of his mechanisms
average and wasteful: in the long range, then,
worms lighten trees and let in light: but that's
another problem: could it be maintained that
the worm lets in light enough
to increase growth equal to his destruction:
     it's a good point, a true variable, but surely
any sudden defoliation by a plague of worms
would be harmful: a re-entry of winter (though possibly
with all of winter's possibility): time and number figure
mysteriously here:

one should be patient and note large results,
reserve some time for broad awareness:

broad awareness is the gift of settled minds: or of
minds hurt high from painful immediacy: it eliminates
and jettisons
sensory contact with too much accident and event—total
     dependencies at the edge: the man
fully aware,
unable to separate out certain large motions, probably
couldn't move: it's better, I think, to be
broadly and emptily aware so as more efficiently
to negotiate the noons of recurrence:

(I have come lately to honor gentleness so:
it's because
of my engagement with
tiny sets and systems of energy, nucleations and constructs,
that I'm unnerved with the slight and needful
     of consideration: part of consideration's
slightness: it approaches and stands off peripherally
quiet and patient should a gesture
be all that's right

but of course it will on invitation tend:
it never blunts or overwhelms with aid
or transforms in order to be received):

while shade increases equally with surface area of leaf
the net result's
a considerable variance:
leaves inter-shade
but the result on the ground's non-accumulative:

in May last year, a month before the above sketch, I did another
briefer thing:

elm seed, maple
seed shower
loose when the wind
stirs, a spring-wind harvesting
(when so many things
have to be picked—take strawberries,
stooped to and crawled
along before, or the finger-bluing
of blueberries):
everything so
gentle and well
done: I sit down not to flaw
the ambience:

the elm seed's winged all round
and exists, a sheathed
swelling, in the center: it
can flutter,
spin,
or, its axis just right, slice
with a draft or cut through one:
(it doesn't go very far but it can
get out of the shade):

then there's the maple seed's oar-wing:
it spins too

(simply, on an ordinary day)
but in a gust can glide broadside:

(dandelion seeds in a head are
noted for their ability to become detached
though attached:
with a tiny splint-break
the wind can have a bluster of them:
the coming fine of an intimation):

those are facts, one-sided extensions:
since the wind's indifferent
the seeds take pains to
make a difference:
praise god for the empty and undesigned:

        hampered by being ungreat poetry, incapable of
carrying quick conviction into imagination's locked clarity,

nevertheless these pieces establish the point
that a book might be written on the interpenetrations of
appearance of an elm tree, especially when the seasons could be

brought in, the fluff cresting snow limbs, the stars and the
influence of starlight on growth or stunting—I have no
idea how such distance affects leaves—the general surround, as of

wind, rain, air pollution, bird shade, squirrel nest: books
by the hundred have already been written on cytology, the
study of cells, and in an elm tree there are twelve quintillion cells,

especially in the summer foliage, and more takes place by way
of event, disposition and such in a single cell than any computer
we now have could keep registration of, given the means of deriving

the information: but if I say books could be written about a single
tree I mean to say only that truth is difficult, even when
noncontradicting; that is, the mere massive pile-up of information

is recalcitrant to higher assimilations without great loss of
concretion, without wide application of averaging: things are
reduced into knowledge: and truth, as some kind of lofty reification,

is so great a reduction it is vanished through by spirit only, a
parallelogram, square or beam of light, or perhaps a more casual
emanation or glow: when so much intellectual energy seems to be

coming to nothing, the mind searches its culture clutch for meaningful
or recurrent objects, finds say a crown or flag or apple or tree or
beaver and invests its charge in that concretion, that focus: then

the symbol carries exactly the syrup of many distillations and
hard endurance, soft inquiry and turning: the symbol apple and the
real apple are different apples, though resembled: "no ideas but in

things" can then be read into alternatives—"no things but in ideas,"
"no ideas but in ideas," and "no things but in things": one thing
always to keep in mind is that there are a number of possibilities:

whatever sways forward implies a backward sway and the mind must
either go all the way around and come back or it must be prepared
to fall back and deal with the lost sway, the pressure for dealing

increasing constantly with forwardness: it's surprising to me
that my image of the orders of greatness comes in terms of descent:
I would call the lyric high and hard, a rocky loft, the slow,

snowline melt of individual crystalline drops, three or four to
the lyric: requires precision and nerve, is almost always badly
accomplished, but when not mean, minor: then there is the rush,

rattle, and flash of brooks, pyrotechnics that turn water white:
poetry is magical there, full of verbal surprise and dashed
astonishment: then, farther down, the broad dealing, the smooth

fullness of the slow, wide river: there starts the show of genius,
in motion, massive beyond the need of disturbing surprise, but, still,
channeled by means—the land's—other than its own: genius, and

the greatest poetry, is the sea, settled, contained before the first
current stirs but implying in its every motion adjustments
throughout the measure: one recognizes an ocean even from a dune and

the very first actions of contact with an ocean say ocean over and
over: read a few lines along the periphery of any of the truly
great and the knowledge delineates an open shore:

what is to be gained from the immortal person except the experience
of ocean: take any line as skiff, break the breakers, and go out
into the landless, orientationless, but perfectly contained, try

the suasions, brief dips and rises, and the general circulations,
the wind, the abundant reductions, stars, and the experience is
obtained: but rivers, brooks, and trickles have their uses and

special joys and achieve, in their identities, difficult absoluteness:
but will you say, what of the content—why they are all made of water:
but will you, because of the confusion, bring me front center as

a mere mist or vapor: charity is greater than poetry: enter it,
in consideration of my need and weakness: I find I am able to say
only what is in my head: a heady constraint: and to say it only

as well as I can: inventory my infirmities and substitute
your love for them, and let us hold on to one another and
move right away from petulant despair: to broach a summary, I

would say the problem is scientific—how is reality to be
rendered: how is 4,444 to be made 444 and 44 and 4 and 1: I
have the shaky feeling I've just said something I don't trust:

poems are arresting in two ways: they attract attention with
glistery astonishment and they hold it: stasis: they gather and
stay: the progression is from sound and motion to silence and

rest: for example, I can sit in this room, close my eyes, and
reproduce the whole valley landscape, still: I can see the
southern end of Lake Cayuga, I can see Stewart Park, the highways,

the breaking out and squaring up of Ithaca, I can see the hill-ridges
rising from the Lake, trees, outcroppings of rocks, falls, ducks
and gulls, the little zoo, the bridges: I can feel my eyesight

traveling around a held environment: I am conscious that the
landscape is fixed at the same time that I can move around in it:
a poem is the same way: once it is thoroughly known, it contains

its motion and can be reproduced whole, all its shapeliness intact,
to the mind at the same time the mind can travel around in it and
know its sound and motion: nothing defined can

be still: the verbal moves, depends there, or sinks into unfocused
irreality: ah, but when the mind is brought to silence, the
non-verbal, and the still, it's whole again to see how motion goes:

the left nest in the shrub has built up a foothigh cone of snow
this morning and four sparrows sitting in the quince bush are
the only unaugmented things around: eight more inches are piling

on to ten we had and every evergreen has found the way it would
lean in a burden, split its green periphery and divide: John's
old tractor on the lawn only shows its steering wheel: the

snowplow's been by and blocked the driveway: it's December 26:
yesterday was Christmas: I got a pair of water-resistant gloves
with a removable woolen lining: I got Phyllis three charms for

the bracelet I bought her in Rome: John got a snowsled, a beautiful
wooden train set, Lincoln logs, toggles, and several things
operated by non-included batteries: this morning he has no fever:

he's had tonsillitis this is the fifth day with fevers to 103 and
104: I've felt built over a jerking machine, not quite turned on
or off: this morning John put on his new cowboy hat (he's nearly

four) and I put on his crash helmet, and we searched all the dark
corners and closets for thieves and robbers: we jailed a couple:
one teddy bear and one stuffed, long-legged leprechaun: everyone

will find here a detail that is a key to a set of memories:
strings of nucleations please me more than representative details:
(not that the detail is representative—only that it is a detail

of numerical dominance in recurrence):

> subatomic particle
> atom
> molecule
> cell
> tissue
> organ
> organ system
> organism
> species
> community
> living world

> > > or

> observation
> problem
> hypothesis
> experiment
> theory
> natural law:

> > > > > the swarm at the
subatomic level may be so complex and surprising that it puts
quasars, pulsars and other matters to shame: I don't know:

and "living world" on the other hand may be so scanty in its
information as to be virtually of no account: nevertheless,
a drift is expressed in the progressions up or down—organization,

the degree of: the control into integration (integrated action)
of the increasingly multiple: the human organism, composed of
billions of cells formed into many specializations and subordinations,

can deliver its total lust to the rarification of sight of the

beloved: for example: and many other high levels of symmetry,
unification, and concerted thrust: poems, of human make, are

body images, organisms of this human organism: if that isn't
so I will be terribly disappointed: it sounds as if it ought to
be right: consonants, vowels, idioms, phrases, clauses (tissues),

sentences (organs), verses (organ systems), poems (living worlds):
I react to such stuff with a burst of assent resembling for all
I can tell valuable feeling: rubbing a girl also, of course,

produces feeling, I would be the last to deny it, but it may be
precisely the organization-principle in girls that one, rubbing,
is pleasured by: if, as I believe, we are not only ourselves—i.e.,

the history of our organism—but also every process that went into
our making, then, in the light of our present ignorance, we may
safely leave much potentiality to undisclosed possibility: mush,

mush, how friendly: that's what I think, I'll tell you in a nut-
shell: and in poems, the insubstantial processes of becoming
form inscrutable parts of the living thing: and then how the

orders of the poem build up and cooperate into the pure heat of
sight and insight, trembling and terror: it makes me gasp aghast:
no wonder we pedants talk about history, influence, meaning

in poems: that's peripheral enough to prevent the commission of
larger error, and safe error is a pedantic preference well-known,
widely footnoted, and amply rewarded: I believe in fun:

"superior amusement" is a little shitty: fun is nice: it's what
our society is built on: fun in the enterprise: I believe in it:
I have no faith in the scoffers: they are party-poopers who are

afraid they ought to believe in history or logical positivism and
don't have any real desire to do so: they are scarcely worth a
haircut: organisms, I can tell you, build up under the thrust to

joy and nothing else can lift them out of the miry circumstance:

and poems are pure joy, however divisionally they sway with grief:
the way to joy is integration's delivery of the complete lode:

the flow broken, coinless, I, the third morning of Ithaca's most
historical snowbind, try to go on, difficult, difficult, the hedges
split open, showing inside the vacancy and naked, bony limbs: snow

up past the garage door handle, new snow still falling, and high
gusts roaring through the cold: supplies low or gone: and the stores
closed: that last appeals too much in the wrong sort: like any

scholar, I should, at this point to uncripple the condition, quote,
but first, I must, like a scholar, clear the field: I choose Ruskin
to say what thousands have said: "Art is neither to be achieved by

effort of thinking, nor explained by accuracy of speaking": well,
still, Ruskin, it cannot be achieved without effort, and one level
of accuracy may be preferred to another: this must be a point of

clustering because I feel a lot of little things jostling
to get in where they can be said: for example, I just walked
a mile to the store, blowing snow, I was in to my ass practically

getting out to the plowed road: I got hotdogs, bacon, bread (out of
eggs), coffee: and on the way back, the wind in my face and snow
drifted ten feet high along one curve that has an open field behind

it, I passed two straggly young girls laughing, dogs barking after
them, and one carrying her jacket, big boobs jouncing in her short-
sleeved sweater: I was barking inside myself a little, rosy ideas

in the blinding snowlight: one guy I passed said "beautiful weather"—
the kind of thing one, after four days penned up, is grateful to
say and hear: I quote now to enrich the mix, to improve my stew from

the refrigerator of timeless ingredients:

> "A large number of the inhabitants of a mud flat will be
> worms. It is hard to develop enthusiasm for worms, but it took
> nature more than a billion years to develop a good worm—

meaning one that has specialized organs for digestion, respi-
ration, circulation of the blood and excretion of wastes.
All organisms perform these functions—amoebas, flagellates,
bacteria or even filterable viruses; but the worms—at least
the higher worms—do all these things better. They also de-
veloped segmentation or reduplication of parts, permitting in-
crease in size with completely coordinated function. Contem-
porary architects call this modular construction. It is found in
man in the spinal column, in the segmental arrangement of
spinal nerves, and in some other features that are especially
prominent during embryonic development."

The Sea by Robert C. Miller. Random House. New York,
1966. p. 165.

"We may sum up. Carbohydrates, fats, proteins, nucleic
acids, and their various derivatives, together with water and
other inorganic materials, plus numerous additional com-
pounds found specifically in particular types of living matter
—these are the molecular bricks out of which living matter is
made. To be sure, a mere random pile of such bricks does not
make a living structure, any more than a mere pile of real
bricks makes a house. First and foremost, if the whole is to be
living, the molecular components must be organized into a
specific variety of larger microscopic bodies; and these in turn,
into actual, appropriately structured cells."

The Science of Botany by Paul B. Weisz and Melvin S.
Fuller. McGraw-Hill Book Company, Inc., 1962. p. 48.

                                        poems are verbal
symbols for these organizations: they imprint upon the mind
examples of integration in which the energy flows with maximum

effect and economy between the high levels of oneness and the
numerous subordinations and divisions of diversity: it is simply
good to have the mind exposed to and reflected by such examples:

it firms the mind, organizes its energy, and lets the controlled
flows occur: that is simple good in itself: I can't stress that
enough: it is not good for something else—although of course

it is good for infinite things else: so my point is that the poem
is the symbolical representation of the ideal organization, whether
the cell, the body politic, the business, the religious

group, the university, computer, or whatever: I used to wonder
why, when they are so little met and understood, poems are taught
in schools: they are taught because they are convenient examples

of the supreme functioning of one and many in an organization of
cooperation and subordination: young minds, if they are to "take
their place in society" need to learn patience—that oneness is

not useful when easily derived, that manyness is not truthful when
thinly selective—assent, that the part can, while insisting on
its own identity, contribute to the whole, that the whole can

sustain and give meaning to the part: and when these things
are beautifully—that is, well—done, pleasure is a bonus
truth-functioning allows: that is why art is valuable: it is

extremely valuable: also, in its changing, it pictures how
organizations can change, incorporate innovation, deal with accidence
and surprise, and maintain their purpose—increasing the means and

assuring the probability of survival: the point of change, though,
brings me to a consideration of the adequacy of the transcendental
vegetative analogy: the analogy is so appealing, so swept with

conviction, that I hardly ever have the strength to question it:
I've often said that a poem in becoming generates the laws of its
own becoming: that certainly sounds like a tree, growing up with

no purpose but to become itself (regardless of the fact that many
are constantly trying to turn it into lumber): but actually, a tree
is a print-out: the tree becomes exactly what the locked genetic

code has pre-ordained—allowing, of course, for variables of weather,
soil, etc.: so that the idea that some organic becoming is
realizing itself in the vegetative kingdom is only partially

adequate: real change occurs along the chromosomes, a risky business
apparently based on accidence, chance, unforeseeable distortion:
the proportion of harmful to potentially favorable mutations is

something like 50,000 to 1: how marvelous that the possibility of
favorable change is a flimsy margin in overwhelming, statistically,
destruction and ruin: that is the way nature pours it on: once it

has arrived at a favorable organization—a white oak, for example—
it does not allow haphazard change to riddle it—no, it protects the
species by the death of thousands of its individuals: but lets the

species buy by the hazard of its individuals the capacity to adjust,
should adjustment be indicated or allowed: that is terrifying and
pleasing: a genetic cull myself, I have the right to both

emotions: along the periphery of integrations, then, is an exposure
to demons, thralls, witcheries, the maelstrom black of
possibility, costly, chancy, lethal, open: so I am not so much

arguing with the organic school as shifting true organismus from
the already organized to the bleak periphery of possibility,
an area transcendental only by its bottomless entropy: a word on the

art/nature thing: art is the conscious preparation for the unconscious
event: to the extent that it is possible—a fining up of the attention
and filling out of the means: art is the craft and lore of preparing

the soil for seed: no enmity: complementary: is any yeoman
dumb enough to think that by much cultivation of the fields wheat
will sprout: or that saying words over the barren, the seedless,

will make potatoes: son of a gun's been keeping a bag of seed-wheat
in the barn all winter, has sorted out good potatoes and knows how
to cut their eyes out: it's hard to say whether the distinguishers

or the resemblancers are sillier: they work with noumena every
day, but speak of the invisible to them and they laugh with
silver modernity: well, as I said, we are more certain that we

are about than what we are about: here is something I have always
wanted to quote:

> "Around the mouths of rivers, where the fresh waters of the
> land meet the salt waters of the sea, live some of the world's
> densest populations. This food-rich borderland harbors
> immense numbers and varieties of living creatures—proto-
> zoans, worms, snails, shrimp, clams, oysters and on up
> through the vertebrate fishes. Life in an estuary may be rich,
> but it is also almost inconceivably dangerous. The temperature
> of its shallow waters runs the scale from freezing to over 100
> degrees Fahrenheit. Twice each day the ebb and flow of the
> tides drastically alter the conditions of life, sometimes strand-
> ing whole populations to die a high-and-dry or freezing death.
> Winds, floods, and tidal currents often bury the stationary
> bottom animals under suffocating slides of sand or silt. But the
> greatest hazard of all is alien water—water that is too fresh
> or too salty. Aquatic animals are sensitive to the salt content
> of their water environment. A sudden rain-fed flood of fresh
> water from a river mouth can be catastrophic to populations
> dwelling in the estuary."

> "The Life of an Estuary" by Robert M. Ingle. *Scientific
> American*, May 1954.

       isn't that beautiful: it has bearing in many
ways on my argument: it provided me years ago with ideas on

risks and possibilities: well, my essay is finished: I thank it
with all my heart for helping me to get through this snowstorm:
having a project is useful especially during natural suspensions.

Extremes and Moderations

Hurly-burly: taking on whatever is about to get off, up the
slack, ready with prompt-copy for the reiteration, electronic
to inspect the fuzzy-buffoon comeback, picking up the diverse
gravel of mellifluous banality, the world-replacing world

world-irradiating, lesser than but more outspoken:
constructing the stanza is not in my case exceedingly
difficult, variably invariable, permitting maximum change
within maximum stability, the flow-breaking four-liner, lattice

of the satisfactory fall, grid seepage, currents distracted
to side flow, multiple laterals that at some extreme spill
a shelf, ease back, hit the jolt of the central impulse: the
slow working-down of careful investigation, the run

diffused, swamped into variable action: my ideal's a cold
clod clam calm, clam contained, nevertheless active in the
digestion, capable of dietary mirth, the sudden whisk, nearly
rollably spherical: ah, but friends, to be turned

loose on an accurate impulse! how handsome the stanzas are
beginning to look, open to the total acceptance, fracturing into
delight, tugging down the broad sweep, thrashing it into
particulars (within boundaries): diversity, however—as of

the concrete—is not ever-pleasing: I've seen fair mounds
of fine-stone at one end or the other of highway construction
many times and been chiefly interested in the "hill": but
abstraction is the bogey-boo of those incapable of it, while,

merrily, every abstractor brings the concrete up fine: one,
anyway, as Emerson says, does well what one settles down to:
it's impossible anyone should know anything about the concrete
who's never risen above it, above the myth of concretion

in the first place: pulverize such, unequal to the synthesis,
the organism by which they move and breathe their particulars:
and the symbol won't do, either: it differentiates flat
into muffling fact it tried to stabilize beyond: there aren't

just problems for the mind, the mind's problematic, residing
here by a scary shading merely: so much so it does seem
at times to prefer an origin other-worldly, the dreaminess,
the surficial hanging-on, those interior swirls nearly

capable of another invention: astonishingly, the
celestial bodies are round, not square or triangular, not
dodecahedral, and then they are sprinkled in the void's
unusual abundance: if it weren't for light, we wouldn't think

anything here, that scanty a fabric: that is the way it
was made: worse, that is the way it works out: when the lady
said she accepted the universe, it was a sort of decision:
anyway, granted that the matter appears to be settled, there's

plenty around for the mind to dwell on: that's a comfort,
but, now, a ghastly comfort: that's the difference:
the first subject I wanted to introduce, because it's
inanimate but highly active, is my marble garden bench down

by the elm—actually, well under the elm: it's in three parts:
the seat slab, four to five inches thick, and the two end slabs,
equally thick but, deeply buried, of undetermined length: I
bought this old place a few years ago, so wasn't present for the

setting: but as to length the upper slab is, say, four feet:
some cool seeps up the legs from the ground, but I
doubt there's much commission between the legs and the upper
slab: cool nights deeply penetrate the bench, so that on

a flash-hot summer morning, the reservoir of dense cooling
will ooze right through to one's bottom, providing, I must say,
a tendency to equilibrium: the stone never gets as hot as the
day and never as cool as the night (maybe it's colder some winter

nights of cold remembrances) so it moderates the environment,
working as a heater or air-conditioner: it has no moving
parts—it's all moving parts, none visible—and yet is
capable of effect, animation: that such a thing can work for

us day and night makes us feel, by cracky, that nature is our
servant, though without singular intention: the gift, though,
the abundance! we don't have to pay for, that requires no
matching social security funds, no fringe benefits: the

unutterable avenue of bliss: in spite of the great many works
in progress, I feel this is the last poem to the world: every
poet probably feels he is writing the last poem to the world:
man, in motion how avaricious, has by the exaggeration of his

refinement shown what intelligence can commit in the universe:
bleak scald of lakes, underground poisonous tides, air litter
like a dusk, clouds not like the clouds: can we give our wild
life a brake: must we keep tinkering until a virus swerves

from our interventions into a genesis consummating us: must
we spew out acids till we're their stew: lead on the highways,
washing into the grass, collecting into lead brooklets bound
for diffusive destinations: get your musclebound mercury dose

here: come on, guys: we know how to handle the overpopulation
problem: sell folks carloads of improvement marked uncertain:
progress can be the end of us: how neat: in a way, you might
say, how right, how just, poetically just: but come on, I say,

overrefined exaggeration, if you got us into this, can't you
get us out: come on, hot-shot fusion: give us plenty with no
bitter aftertaste: paradise lies ahead, where it's always lain:
but we may reach it, before hell overtakes us: nature, if I may

judge out a law, likes extremes, in some ways depends on them, but
usually keeps them short or confined: if we are broadly, densely
extreme, can't we count on the outbreak of dialectical alternatives:
we can count on it: what is a beer party now but a can of cans:

what is wine now but a bottle in a recalcitrant green glow,
empurpling in the sun: nevertheless, the petunias are incarnadine
by the hedgebrush: nevertheless, the catbird comes to the plastic
boat the goldfish summers in, fools around looking, then takes

a drink: we are aided by much I will discuss and much as
yet unfixed: it's time I introduced an extreme, but this time
I'm going to pick a moderate one, I think—the gusts before
thunderstorms: now the gusts before thunderstorms are sometimes

high enough to trim trees: a bough summer has coaxed overweight,
that splitting riddance, serviceable enough, but more anthropo-
centrically, the shaking out of dead branches: when we are
out walking in the woods on a calm day, we don't want a

dead limb to just plunge out of a tree by surprise, striking us,
possibly, on the cranium: whatever we normally go to the woods
for, surely we don't go for that: by high gusts thunderstorms
accomplish the possibility of calm residence: the tree, too,

counts on nodding times, sun-gleanings, free of astonishment,
and to buy them is willing to give up its dead or
even its living limbs: nature gives much on occasion
but exacts a toll, a sacrifice: that puzzling suggestion,

or autumnal impulse, has accounted for much sacred carnage: I
hate to think of it: I nearly hate to think of it: the Maya
hearts pulled out still flicking have always seemed to me gruesome
separations, attention-getting, but god-like with revulsion's awe:

of course, even closer home, high gusts can carry hints to the
hapless by, for example, blowing down a fence obviously too weak
to stand: that should be good news to the farmer whose cows have
been getting out: and who should not be alarmed by an immediate

problem if the lesson has been well bestowed: nature sometimes
gets all its shit together and lets you have it: but good farmers
make good fences and anybody else gets whatever the traffic will
bear away: I wrote the other day a poem on this subject:

Ancestors

An elm tree, like a society or
culture, seems to behave out of
many actions toward a total
interest (namely, its own) which means
that in the clutter and calamity
of days much, locally catastrophic,
can occur that brings no sharp
imbalance to the total register:
for example, dead limbs, white already
with mold and brackets, can in
a high storm—the heralding windtwists
of thunderstorms, say—snap and, though
decay-light, plunge among the
lower greens, the many little stiff
fingers entangling, weighing down
the structures of growth: ah, what
an insupportable extravagance by
the dead, held off the ground, leaching
white with slow, dry rot: what
a duty for the young limbs, already
crowding and heavy with green: well,
I guess the elm is by that much local
waste wasted, but then perhaps its
sacrifice is to sway in some deep rich
boughs the indifferent, superfluous,
recalcitrant, white, prophesying dead.

circulations are moderations, currents triggered by extremes:
we must at all costs keep the circulations free and clear,
open and unimpeded: otherwise, extremes will become trapped,
local, locked in themselves, incapable of transaction: some

extremes, though, *are* circulations, a pity, in that kinds of
staying must then be the counters: for example, when in spring
a gray sandstorm arises over Indiana, circulation becomes
too free and open: hedgerows, even, are important at such times:

they stall the storm just enough for heavy sand to fall out:
but what of the lengthy problem of small sand and, even worse,
of high-rising fine dust: if the storm hits
Pennsylvania, the woods will drag at its foot, then

tilt and capitulate it: heavy suspensions will lose their
directions to gravity quickly but even the fine dust slowing will
sift through the equally numerical leaves, be caught by them,
and the air will be breatheable again by Jersey, west Jersey:

water's carriages act the same way: high narrow valleys, roomless,
propel water along, loosening sometimes substantial boulders: the
mature valleys, wide-bottomed, slow the flow, and
particulate weight falls out: in the ancient flat valleys,

where meanders have cut off into oxbow lakes or little crescents
of difference, the water goes broad and slow and only the
fine stuff in a colloidal float, a high drift, stays out
the ride, hanging finally in long curtains in the gulfs and lagoons:

well, I just, for poetic purposes, wanted to point out the parallel:
parallel too in that even Pennsylvania can't get some of the
high dust, the microscopic grit—settles out with the
floating spiders on Atlantic isles and (too bad for the spiders)

waves: such circulations are average and quite precious: the
sun's the motor, the mechanisms greased by millions of years
of propriety and correction: the place produced deliciously
habitable, a place we found we could grow into: how marvelous!

lightning is one of the finest, sharpest tensions, energy
concentrations: it has to be lean because it leaps far:
how was the separation to be bridged, the charge neutralized,
except by a high-energy construct: gathers the diffuse

energy from clouds and ground and drains it through a
dense crackling: I don't know how it works: it works:
the charges rush together and annihilate each other:
or the charge goes one way, to the ground, or to the

clouds: I'll bet it's one way and to the ground: the
lofted's precarious: the ground is nice and sweet and not
at all spectacular: I wonder if I'm really talking about
the economy of the self, where an extreme can gather up a lot

of stale stuff and mobilize it, immoderate grief,
or racing terror, or a big unification like love chugging
up to the fold: we never talk about anything but ourselves,
objectivity the objective way of talking about ourselves:

O calligraphers, blue swallows, filigree the world
with figure, bring the reductions, the snakes unwinding,
the loops, tendrils, attachments, turn in necessity's precision,
give us the highwire of the essential, the slippery concisions

of tense attentions! go to look for the ocean currents and
though they are always flowing there they are, right in place, if
with seasonal leans and sways: the human body
staying in change, time rushing through, ingestion,

elimination: if change stopped, the mechanisms of
holding would lose their tune: current informs us,
is the means of our temporary stay: ice water at the northern
circle sinks and in a high wall like a glacier seeps down the

ocean bottom south: but the south's surface water is going
north, often in spiral carriages of an extreme intensity, nevertheless
moderating, preventing worse extremes: as when snow streaks up the
summit, up past the timberline where interference is slight, and

having passed the concision of the ridge, blooms out diffusing
over the valley, drifts out into the catchments, fills with
feathery loads the high ravines, the glacier's compressions forming
underneath, taking direction in the slowest flow of relief, so on

any number of other occasions, massive collections and dispositions
restore ends to sources: O city, I cry at
the gate, the glacier is your
mother, the currents of the deep father you, you sleep

in the ministry of trees, the boulders are your brothers sustaining
you: come out, I cry, into the lofty assimilations: women, let
down your hair under the dark leaves of the night grove, enter
the currents with a sage whining, rising into the circular

dance: men, come out and be with the wind, speedy and lean, fall
into the moon-cheered waters, plunge into the ecstasy of rapids:
children, come out and play in the toys of divinity: glass, brick,
stone, curb, rail are freezing you out of your motions, the

uncluttered circulations: I cry that, but perhaps I am too secular
or pagan: everything, they say, is artificial: nature's the
artwork of the Lord: but your work, city, is aimed unnaturally
against time: your artifice confronts the Artifice: beyond

the scheduled consummation, nothing's to be recalled: there is
memory enough in the rock, unscriptured history in
the wind, sufficient identity in the curve
of the valley: what is your name, city, under your name: who

are your people under their faces: children of the light,
children of the light: of seasons, moons, apples, berries,
grain: children of flies, worms, stars: come out, I cry, into
your parentage, your established natures: I went out and pulled a

few weeds in the lawn: you probably think I was getting goofy
or scared: it was just another show: as the mystic said, it's
all one to me: then I went on over to the University, and there
was Slatoff's new book, fresh from the publisher's: and Kaske

had left me a book he'd told me about: *Ballad of the Bones
and Other Poems*, by Byron Herbert Reece: E.P. Dutton: 1945:
$2.00: introduced by Jesse Stuart: and praised, on
the back cover, by William Rose Benet, John Hall Wheelock,

John Gould Fletcher, and Alfred Kreymborg: I do believe I'm going
to enjoy the book: the South has Mr. Reece and, probably,
Literature: I bet I pulled a thousand weeds: harkweed's
incredible: it puts up a flower (beautiful) to seed but at the

same time sends out runners under the grass that anchor a few
inches or a foot away, and then the leaves of the new plants
press away the grass in a tight fit: I put havoc into those
progressions, believe me: plants take their cue and shape

from crowding: they will crowd anything, including close
relatives, brethren and sistren: everybody, if I may switch
tracks, is out to get his: that is the energy we must allow
the widest margin to: and let the margins, then, collide into

sensible adjustments: slow moderations are usually massive:
nature can't heave a lot fast, air and
oceans reasonably unwieldy: true, they work into lesser
intensities, local: maelstroms, typhoons, fairly rapid highs

or lows, the boiling up of deep, cold water: dimension may be
the sorter, although it didn't seem so originally with the
garden bench, small and yet efficiently moderating: if
you built a wall across the Gulf Stream, though, the sundering

would be lengthy: and what would it take to bring about a quick
thermal change in an ocean: a solar burst; at least,
unusual effusion: quantity of mass or number (as of leaves) then
moderates the local effect: as for cooling an ocean, a lot of

icebergs would have to split off from the caps and plunge before
the change would be measurable: expanded, though, through
sufficient time—a massiveness—the lesser effects could assume
large implications: but, of course, with the icebergs, one

would have to investigate the mechanisms that were heating up the
general air, causing the splits in the first place, and then one
would have to deal with the probability that the air, massive to
massive, would warm up the oceans which would then be able to

absorb large numbers of icebergs without cooling: I suppose
my confusion is no more than natural, reflecting
the reticulation of interpenetration in nature, whereby we should
be advised to tamper cautiously with least balances,

lest a considerable number, a series or so, tilt
akimbo: even now, though, we apparently cannot let well enough
alone: how well it was! how computer-like in billionths the
administration and take of the cure: just think, the best cure

would arise by subtle influence of itself if only we would
disappear: but though we have scalded and oiled the seas and
scabbed the land and smoked the mirror of heaven, we must try
to stay and keep those who are alive alive: then we

might propose to ourselves that collectively we have one grain
of sense and see what the proposition summons forth: the force of
the drive by which we have survived is hard to counter, even
now that we survive so densely: and it is not certain the plants

would not lose their shape and vigor if they had to stop
crowding: a very hard reversal and loss of impetus: we may
have time to diminish and cope with our thrust: the little patch
of wildwoods out behind my backhedge is even now squeaky and

chirpy with birds and the day is as clear as a missing windowpane:
the clouds are few, large, and vastly white: the air has no
smell and the shade of trees is sharp: floods are extreme
by narrowing rain, which can, itself, be quite bountiful:

it's hard to blame floods—useless—because they're just
showing how hard they can work to drain the land:
one way a slow impulse works up into an extremity's
the earthquake: coastal land, say, drifts with sea currents

north a couple of inches a year, setting up a strain along a
line with the land's land: at some point, tension gives in
a wrack and wrecks stability, restoring lassitude: or resonance
of circulation coming into a twist or "beat": the gathering up,

the event, the dissipation: but that would imply that everything,
massive, slow, or long is moving toward the enunciation of
an extreme: we dwell in peace on the post-tables and
shelves of these remarkable statements: what kind of lurch is

it, I wonder, when a comet sideswipes us, or swishes by near
enough to switch our magnetic poles: can the atmosphere
be shifted a few hundred miles: the oceans
would pile up and spill: maybe just the magnetic poles would

switch, that sounds all right: but if the comet hit us and
glanced off or even stuck, its impact would affect
our angular momentum and possibly put some wobble in our motion:
somebody said the purpose of science is to put us in control

of our environment, allaying calamity and catastrophe, though
conceivably also making nice days a little nicer: well, all
I say (figuratively speaking) is a lot of things are
still in their own control: maybe my point, though, is that

by and large I prefer the other controls to our own, not
forsaking the possibility that still larger controls
by us might bring about a fair, if slightly artificialized,
paradise someday: from here, it looks like ruin and

destruction either way, more or less: one thing we will never
do is sit around on this planet doing nothing, just soaking
up the honey of solar radiation: if our problems were
solved, we'd go out of business: (stretch that a little

and it will do): it's dry: the weeds in the lawn
are being tested to the limit, some having died: I've just
put a soakhose by the maple: I'll let it go slowly that way
for a few hours: the grass in patches is parched tan:

it crackles underfoot: tight spurs of hay:
I didn't see the hornet at first when I went to attach the
hose: he was sucking the spigot: people around here don't
have sprinklers, I can't understand it: I always used to have

one in South Jersey: maybe water's expensive or maybe
very dry spells are rare: seems to me I remember a very dry
one last year: the days are shortening: it's sundown
now at eight: maybe a little later officially, but the sun's

down behind the ridge on the other side of the lake by then: any
night could turn sharp cold—read August 21: I've been at this
poem or prose-poem or versification or diversification for three
or four days: I'll never get all the weeds

out of the grass: I just know after each day that
there are a hell of a lot fewer weeds in the lawn:
it's evening: seven: I just noticed
a dark cloud coming from the west, so I went out

and said, please, rain some here: a few pin drops
fell, I think though more because of the dark cloud than the
saying: saying doesn't do any good but it doesn't
hurt: aligns the psychic forces with the natural:

that alignment may have some influence: I have found the world
so marvelous that nothing would surprise me: that may sound
contradictory, the wrong way to reach the matter-of-fact: but
if you can buy comets sizzling around in super-elongated

orbits and a mathematics risen in man that corresponds to the
orbits, why, simple as it is finally, you can move on to glutinous
molecules sloshing around in the fallen seas for something
to stick to: that there should have been possibilities enough to

include all that has occurred is beyond belief, an extreme the
strictures and disciplines of which prevent loose-flowing
phantasmagoria: last night in the cloud-darkened dusk rain began
gently, the air so full of moisture it just couldn't help it,

and continued at least past midnight when I went to bed: this
morning is dark but not raining: recovery's widespread: rain
comes all over everything: trees, bushes, beans, petunias,
weeds, grass, sandboxes, garages: yesterday I went with the hose

on the hard crusty ground from one single scorched patch to
another, never able to stay long at one point the other places
were calling so hard: ocean dumping of nuclear garbage requires
technological know-how, precision of intention, grace of

manipulation: devilish competition invades even the dirty work
of the world, where, though, the aggressive, intelligent young man
can negotiate spectacular levels of promotion: we have spilt
much energy generating concentrations—nerve gas, specific

insecticides, car polish, household cleansers "fatal if swallowed"—
we must depend on land, sea, and air to diffuse into harmlessness:
but some indestructibles resist all transformation and anyway
our vast moderators are limited: an oil slick covers every inch

of ocean surface: at the poles pilots see in the contrast the
sullied air's worldwide: because of the circulations, water can
never be picked up for use except from its usages, where what
has gone in is not measured or determined: extreme calls to

extreme and moderation is losing its quality, its effect: the
artificial has taken on the complication of the natural and where
to take hold, how to let go, perplexes individual action: ruin
and gloom are falling off the shoulders of progress: blue-green

globe, we have tripped your balance and gone into exaggerated
possession: this seems to me the last poem written to the world
before its freshness capsizes and sinks into the slush: the
rampaging industrialists, the chemical devisers and manipulators

are forging tanks, filling vats of smoky horrors because of
dollar lust, so as to live in long white houses on the summits
of lengthy slopes, for the pleasures of making others spur and
turn: but common air moves over the slopes, and common rain's

losing its heavenly clarity: if we move beyond
the natural cautions, we must pay the natural costs, our every
extreme played out: where we can't create the room of

playing out, we must avoid the extreme, disallow it: it's Sunday

morning accounts for such preachments, exhortations, and
solemnities: the cumulative vent of our primal energies is now and
always has been sufficient to blow us up: I have my ventilator
here, my interminable stanza, my lattice work that lets the world

breeze unobstructed through: we could use more such harmless
devices: sex is a circular closure, permitting spheric
circularity above hemispheric exchange: innocent, non-destructive,
illimitable (don't you wish it) vent: I want to close (I may

interminably do it, because a flatness is without beginning,
development, or end) with my chief concern: if contaminated
water forces me to the extreme purification of bottled or distilled
water, the extreme will be costly: bulldozers will have to clear

roads to the springs: trucks will have to muck the air to bring
the water down: bottles will have to be made from oil-fired
melts: a secondary level of filth created to escape the first:
in an enclosure like earth's there's no place to dump stuff off.

Hibernaculum

I

A cud's a locus in time, a staying change, moving
but holding through motions timeless relations,
as of center to periphery, core-thought to consideration,

not especially, I'd say, goal-directed, more
a slime- and sublime-filled coasting, a repeating of
gently repeating motions, blissful slobber-spun webs:

today's paper says that rain falls on the desert and makes
it fertile: semen slips, jets, swims into wombs
and makes them bulge: therefore, there must be

2

a big penis above the clouds that spills the rain:
that is, I think, reasonable, which says something for
reason operating in fictions akilter: reason's no

better off than its ambience, and an ambience can't
alter frequently from its reason: (somewhere, though,
along the arm of a backwoods spiral, interchange

and adjustment with the environment are possible but
adjustment likely to be at the surprise of reason,
displeasure included: but then there has to be

3

protection against jolt-change: smashing alterations,
kind of cottonpicking conniptions, fail of impulse:)

the thunderbolt, another celestial phallus, though

sterile, peels trees, explodes bushes, ravels roots,
melds sand into imitation lightning, spurry and branchy,
deep into the ground: that sort of thing is

not promising, so represents, as with Zeus, authority:
cussed superegomaniacal threat that gets from the outside
in, doing its dirty work bitterest closest to

4

pleasure's fundament: the better it feels, the bigger
the bludgeon: O merciful constructions that are so made,
do have mercy: the stuff is sweet, why crud it up

with crud: for every fructifying heavenly penis, such as
the rain penis, a ghastly one seres sand:
if there were any way to get around the universe, somebody

would've by now: history informs despair:
the lucky young, they don't know anybody's screwed
or perished before: just as well, too: although

5

screwing is nearly worth perishing, and, too, the two not
always concomitant: perhaps, co-terminous: but then the
penis is also (like the heavens) splitting and pleasuring:

while it's in, it is, afterall, commanding and will not,
just because somebody's edgy, withdraw: it will come
out only when it backs off from a puzzled loss or when

something truly spectacular appears, a shotgun or, more
accurately, roused maiden aunt: rhythms, speeding up,
build necessity into their programs: I see filigrees of

6

confabulation, curlicues, the salt walking-bush, ah, I see
aggregates of definition, plausible emergences, I see
reticulations of ambience: the days shorten down to a

gap in the night, winter, though gray and vague, not half
dubious enough: I see a sleet-filled sky's dry freeze:
I see diggings disheveled, bleak mounds, burnt openings:

what do I see: I see a world made, unmade, and made again
and I hear crying either way: I look to the ground for the
lost, the ground's lost: I see grime, just grime, grain,

7

grit, grist: the layers at thousand-year intervals
accumulate, reduce to beginnings: but I see the nightwatchman
at the cave's mouth, his eyes turned up in stunned amusement

to the constellations: from zero to zero we
pass through magnificence too shatterable: sight, touch,
inquiring tongue, water spinning into white threads over rocks:

I see the man moving boldly, staking his love on time, time
the slippery, the slick mound stragglers slide into the
everlasting encompassing waters from: not a drop of water

8

hasn't endured the salt-change of change: how
have the clouds kept fresh, the soil kept lively, its
milling microbes, how has the air, drawn into numberless

dyings kept clarity, breatheability: I see quiet lakes
and composed hills: I see the seasonal wash of
white and green: I am alarmed with acceptance: nothing

made right could have been made this way, and nothing
made otherwise could have been made right: nothing can
be made to make it right: we're given the works to

9

purchase nothing: the hardest training of the eye
against this loveliness, what can we make of holding so
to what we must give up, as if only in the act of giving

up can we know the magnificence, spent: what are we
here to learn: how to come into our estates before night
disinherits us: dear God (or whatever, if anything, is

merciful) give us our lives, then, the full possession,
before we give them back: I see the flood-child astir in the
surf, the clouds slowing and breaking into light:

10

what did he buy or sell: what is the meaning of loss
that never lived into gain: the mother, not far off,
flickers in a ditch to the minor winds: how far off

she is, past all touch and dream, the child huddled
snug into himself, his decomposition: how the dark
mind feeds on darkness, hungry for the inmost core: but

it is only darkness, empty, the hollow, the black, sucking
wind: this everyone knows: everyone turns away: light,
tendril, moon, water seize our attention, make us turn:

11

I think we are here to give back our possessions before
they are taken away: with deliberate mind to say to
the crushing love, I am aware you are here cloaked in

this moment, you are priceless, eternity is between us,
we offer ourselves in the sacrifice of time to this

moment become unconditioned and time-evering: I think

we are here to draw the furthest tailing of time round
into the perishing of this purest instant: to make out
the proximity of love to a hundred percent and to zero:

1 2

I see the bitterest acquiescence, the calm eye in the
tragic scene, the smile of the howling mind: I keep
forgetting—I am not to be saved: I keep forgetting this

translation from fleshbody to wordbody is leaving my
flesh behind, that I *have* entered into the wordbody but
may not enter in, not at last: I need a set of practices,

a mnemonics, my fleshbody can keep close to its going:
of those practices the stepping out into love, motion's
glimpse, blanches to the highest burn: I can lose myself:

1 3

I'm not so certain I can lose you, I'm not so certain
you can lose me: but all the others have succeeded, all
the others have tricked on their legs by graves, all

the others have gotten through all the losses and left
the air clear, the bush aleaf, the ground in scent:
after it takes place, there will be a clearing for us,

too, we will be in the wind what shape a leaf would take
if a leaf were there: let's join to the deepest slowing,
turn the deepest dark into touch, gape, pumping, at the

1 4

dark beyond reach: afterwards, shoveling the driveway,
warming up the coffee, going to the grocery store, opening
the cookie jar, washing, shaving, vacuuming, looking out

the window at the perilously afflicted, that is, snow-loaded
bent evergreens, watching the pheasants walking across
the yard, plopping up belly-deep in snow, wondering

if one can get the car out or, out, in: the Ceremony of
Puzzling over the Typewriter, of swishing off the dishes
and getting them in the washer, of taking out the trash

15

and hearing the trash-can lids snap and bang, opened or
squeezed shut: the considerable distance the universe
allows between brushing the teeth and helping John put

his fort together: these small actions near the center
form the integrations, the gestures and melodies, rises
and falls minutes give over to hours, hours to days, days

to weeks, months, and years: it all adds up to zero only
because each filled day is shut away, vanished: and what
memory keeps it keeps in a lost paradise: the heroic

16

entangler, benign arachnid, casting threads to catch,
hang and snatch, draw up the filamental clutch, the
clump-core reticulate, to tie energy into verbal knots

so that only with the death of language dies the energy!
so all the unravellers may feed! the dissipators go with
some grain to their swill: pleasure to my tribe and

sufficient honor! to lean belief the lean word comes,
each scope adjusted to the plausible: to the heart
emptied of, by elimination, the world, comes the small

17

cry domesticating the night: if the night is to be

habitable, if dawn is to come out of it, if day is ever
to grow brilliant on delivered populations, the word

must have its way by the brook, lie out cold all night
along the snow limb, spell by yearning's wilted weed till
the wilted weed rises, know the patience and smallness

of stones: I address the empty place where the god
that has been deposed lived: it is the godhead: the
yearnings that have been addressed to it bear antiquity's

18

sanction: for the god is ever re-created as
emptiness, till force and ritual fill up and strangle
his life, and then he must be born empty again: I

accost the emptiness saying let all men turn their
eyes to the emptiness that allows adoration's life:
that is my whole saying, though I have no intention to

stop talking: our immediate staying's the rock but
the staying of the rock's motion: motion, that spirit!
we could veer into, dimpling, the sun or into the cold

19

orbital lofts, but our motion, our weight, our speed
are organized here like a rock, our spiritual stay:
the blue spruce's become ponderous with snow: brief

melt re-froze and knitted ice to needles and ice
to snow so the ridges eight inches high hold: the
branches move back and forth, stiff wailers:

the cloud-misty moonlight fills small fields, plots,
woodnooks with high light, snow transluminant as
fire: the owl, I'll bet, looks about little from

20

those branchy margins, his eye cleaned of liking in
the soft waste not a mouse burrows or thrashes through,
liking gone inward and sharp into the agony of imagined

mouseful lands: one thing poetry could be resembled to is
soup: the high moving into clarity of quintessential
consomme: then broth, the homogeneous cast of substance's

shadow: then the falling out of diversity into specific
identity, carrot cube, pea, rice grain: then the chunky
predominance of beef hunk, long bean, in heavy gravy:

21

last night the eaves from roof heat dripped and the
drops in those close-holding freezing laminations
noded the tips of the cedar lobes hammer heavy, such

ice: today, though, some sunshine and in the mid-forties,
the freeing up has been steady, if slow: the blue
spruce stands isolated out in the yard—nothing drips

on it except the sky—and since mid-morning it has
had a little melt-shower in it, a shower canopy:
from a low-hung dangle the emptied branches have risen

22

to near horizontal and the snow left looks edged and
drained: I think in the marked up annals of recorded
evolutionary history mind will turn out to have been

nova-like, say; a pressure of chance built up
nature had to take, the slide toward the slow explosion
of searching risk: some think mind will continue

growing out of nature until possessed of its own self
second-nature it will bespeak its own change, turn with
or against the loam out of which it grew: I'm pessimistic:

23

for my little faith, such as it is, is that mind and
nature grew out of a common node and so must obey common
motions, so that dickering with second-nature mind

violates the violation: a made mind can live compre-
hendingly only in a made world and artifice, exact and
independent as it looks, can't, I'll bet, extend intricacy

working out through the core of every single atom: I
depend on the brook to look out where it's going:
I depend on the snow to ornament the woods: I depend

24

on the sun to get up every morning rightfully off-time:
I depend on the sea current to find just which way to
sway to the thermodynamic necessity: I depend utterly

on my body to produce me, keep me produced, don't you:
the autonomy of the mind! who could desire it, staying
up all night to keep the liver right, the pancreas calm:

I prefer like the sweet brook to be at ease with my
findings: I prefer the strictures that release me into
motion: for not even the highest branch is free to wave,

25

it responds as freedom to the wind's tyranny: what have
I to desire of autonomy except slavery, its ware:
I prefer to be offered up by all the designs and musculatures

into the liberty of correspondent motions: when the
mind can sustain itself it then may consider sustaining
the universe: meanwhile, I have nothing, nothing to sell:

I write what is left to write after everything's sold out:
and also I write not very wide, just to the fence or hedge
around the lot (sometimes from my window I take in the

26

neighboring lady's scrap of woods—I hope she
doesn't get word and charge me) but of course I write
straight up and down as far either way as I can reach,

which by sight (but not reach) one way is far but by
reach the other way, the ground, is near, if so opaque
only imagination, that frail, filters through: still

it's world enough to take my time, stretch my reason, hinder
and free me: do a section on the garage roof snow and you
will find several strata: I haven't looked but I know

27

because I was here when they happened: fluff snow, grit
snow, plain sleet, fluff snow, wet snow, more grit, and
snow (regular): similar sedimentary phenomena might be

expected elsewhere: and I have sat here by the window today
and seen a direct relation between the sunny intervals and
the rate of eave-melt off the garage: that close a

pull between the sun and my garage snow stuns me,
though I would be the last to insist it do a thing for you:
I really do not want to convince anyone of anything except

28

that conviction is cut loose, adrift and aswim, upon the
cool (sometimes sweltering) tides of roiling energy:
that's not to despise conviction, definition, or other

structure but to put them in their place: I hope
you are in the middle income bracket (at least): I
desire to be in the very high upper high outgo bracket:

to furnish forth energy out of nothing, except reflection,
a few hard years, several procedures of terror and
astonishment, New Hope Elementary School, assorted

29

mothers and fathers (with the one and the one), fifty
acres of ground, half swamp, half hill, Whiteville High
School, the Pacific Ocean, a small sweep through the arc

of the galaxy, one arm of the spiral in particular,
etc.: I know I can't give all that back but so what I
haven't quit trying yet and anyway it's just giving

nothing to nothing: I'm somewhat shocked by clouds
of organic compounds in deep space but anticipate
no flagrant reaction: I think it's going to rain:

30

our young don't believe in time as future and, so,
suffer every instant's death: they don't believe
in the thread, plot, the leading of one thing into

another, consequence, developed change: without retrospect
or prospect, they seek the quality of experience
a moment's dimension allows: thrill replaces

goal: threat lessens and fractures time, shortening
the distance to the abyss, immediate, a step away:
without calm, they can't see tomorrow unfolding: the mind,

31

too, can't move beyond the surface event into the
assimilations of higher, restful suasions where arc-like
staying has beginning and end and smooth curvature

reliable: hell is the meaninglessness of stringing out
events in unrelated, undirected sequences: remove danger
(holocaust, suffocation, poisoning) from the young and

their anxieties will unwind into long reaches of easeful
seeking: not that anyone is, has been, or ever will be
more than a hair away from disaster, and the statistics

32

on anyone's living forever are unpromising: still,
we have now a Myth of Disaster, and that's harder than
some other kinds of myth: with another snow coming, we

drove out past Route 13 on North Hanshaw this afternoon
to the tree farm for a scotch pine: there was half an
acre of perfectly spaced trees tied up to permanent

stakes: that was enough, some of the stakes deserted:
nevertheless, I bought a full, short, four-dollar tree
which I've just put twinkle lights on: now, with

33

the snow still steady, John and Robbie (his little
friend) are doing their part, hanging balls and
icicles: christmas is still five days away, but no

matter—anticipation starts to burst out of little boys
early, and a present to raising the tree must be opened:
vent, vent: we need every trigger and valve we can

invent to achieve restless deflations: invent vents:
my enormous, airy self sputters like a balloon at its
inadequate outlet and shoots off spinning enlarging circles

34

into the galaxy—or at least over the fence and treetops or
halfway over the lake: when it gets too dry around here
in the summer sometimes, the little creeks nearly creak

with drought, a dribble of a drop dropping off the
dry ledges: well, I could use a little of that spareness
of form and volume: imagine the luxurious lassitude of

taking five minutes to swell into a drop and then let
go with a lengthy reluctance: the last drop bulbing
from the spent member: but little boys have small

35

emotional bladders and the pressure's terrific: they'd
rather have a string of little wow's every day
than build up to one big blast: I see the gully-wash,

lineated at the bottom with every stone the flash
could reach and roll into marcation: the honeybee sings
by the hard cactus, wings, spines, works his way up to

the barrel-tip blossom wet, resilient with the roothair
aperture of giving: somewhere in a dry trunk, the grog-rich
honey cushioning the beeswax: I see the industry of water

36

variously dense and laden, the distributions, the little
pools, saved lockets: the bead in the ant belly,
the thread in a cactus vein, the reservoirs of birds'

eyes: the droplet concentrations: I keep thinking
I'm saved, a shock of mild hilarity! I keep thinking
I'm a pot eternity is dropping coins in! think,

if you will, of that: or I keep thinking these words
translate me into another body less affected by
the weather and time's clicking subtractions:

37

public, I have nothing to say to you, nothing: except,
look at the caterpillar under this clump of grass: it
is fuzzy: look at the sunset: it is colorful: listen:

it's hard to compete here in winter: snow makes the
broadest impression, an ineradicable eradication: slows
and muffles: you can hear the snow fall, a fizz: if

I cannot look at you, I can look with you: since there
is something between us, let it be a thing we share:
if there is nothing between us, I'm coming up with this:

38

by the time I got the world cut down small enough that
I could be the center of it, it wasn't worth having:
but when I gave up center, I found I was peripherally

no bigger than a bit: now, I have decided the former
was the better: I must re-mount the center and force
the world to subside about me: not easy and not

promising, but neither is surrender: still, St. Francis
said if you give up everything it's all yours: giving
up is not easy at all: why is everything so perplexing:

39

I feel in the company of the soul, however, nervous:
I grow arch and curt: I talk nasty: I wink and grunt or
switch to salacity: I mouth reprovables: I don't

belong here, I try to announce: I am not worthy: I say
to the soul, you know this is no place for me: I am,
besides impolite, flawed: but the soul absorbs my defense

and turns my pain into a pure form of itself, investing
my embarrassment with grace: I go out to the hedge bush-vine,
but there is the soul, tangled with curvature: I look at

40

the gaunt maple, but a nest is hung in it: I look
at the points of the picket fence, but there, too, the
snowflakes hold: in between, thinner than sight,

returns and compliances give and take: can I take this
in, I ask, stand with it, assume it: can I talk of it just
as it stalls against the garage, bends upward and outward

around the eaves, picks up a drift and walks it to the edge:
is there an accepting it so complete it vanishes, my wills
and motions tidings in a tide: ah, soul, I say,

41

awkwardness is being conscious of you: I will move and
do directly as I like and that way correspond to your
liking: the point is just to get this page full so I can

take it out of the typewriter and write some letters: sour
cream, yogurt, cottage cheese, chip dip: lizard,
lick-flicking: rancher, ranching: fly, buzzing: tiger,

hassling: cicada, burr-grinding: squirrel, leaping:
chicken, walking: fur, flying: day, breaking: dove,
alighting: fish, gulping: sight, seeing: nose, running:

42

a poem variable as a dying man, willing to try anything,
or a living man, with the consistency of either direction:
just what the mind offers to itself, bread or stone:

in the swim and genesis of the underlying reality things
assume metes and bounds, survive through the wear
of free-being against flux, then break down to swim and

genesis again: that's the main motion but several
interturns have been concocted to confuse it: for example,
the human self risks chaos by breaking down to a flash of

43

single cells in order to plant the full human code early
in the beginning: and many other continuities of pattern,
as slowed flux, work through the flux durably: adagio

in furioso: a slow bass line to a treble revel: tell
him he is lost, he will turn in there and show you what
lost is, a positive sight: tell him his iciness is perfect,

he will lower the cold till perfection drifts like sleep
to aimless absoluteness: tell him he is thin, he will
become so thin the spiritual will take charge: he will

44

turn into any failure abruptly as into a detour and find
his way to a highway: tell him he knows beauty,
he will, going and trying, disclose ugliness: virtue is

waiting anywhere to be by concision of dealing established:
chiefly in the virtueless: huntsman, huntsman, how many
hounds arunning: a lead-hound and a following:

breaking, moving, and filling: people who dress up like
artists, their art form is dressing up like artists:
the sun came up this morning without clouds before it:

45

what is it, then, that the poem is trying to give us
an image of: the ideal image of the ideal man: invariably:
the realist wants to know ideally the ideal realist: the

ragged man and the ragged poem aspire to ideal raggedness:
the loose or fragmented or scopy: the mind can't conceive
any way except into the desired image, the ideal, that's

the only way it works right: let there be, he said
prayerfully though he was only talking, more mass and less
direction, so that the propaganda cannot get off the pad

46

and the concision cannot gather to incision and the
over-simplification cannot settle real clear, accumulative
diversity a dreadnought bristling stifled guns: let

there be, he continued, orb-gathered complication, fuzzy,
bewildering, so that right carries a heavy bilge of wrong
and wrong looks as if it could sump out right: let—

he moved to the rostrum—certainty wallow iceberg-deep in
confusion: let nobody know very much precisely about
anything in—here, puzzled, he dozed: take that lady:

47

her mind is always lying down pleasing the legions: it is
a bow leant in a corner, gaunt with decommission:
how long did that last last last: it's snowing now with

the sun shining: squalls with clearings: today is Tues-
day: yesterday there were 9 hrs and 2 minutes of
daylight, sunup to sundown: that means light is

broadening: right here at the edge of winter-beginning's
winter-ending: today will probably be 9 hrs and 3 minutes:
tomorrow will be different, maybe 9 hrs and 4 minutes:

48

what is the prevailing tone: are there minutes of the
last meeting: should articles be padded with dummy
footnotes: are there any concepts to circulate: can

anyone form a motion: if we stall, will we sink:
if we run, will thinness split underfoot: the mind's
one: it pre-existed, I think: even before it was

mind it was mind plausible: it was the earth: when
it is fully born, it will be another earth, just like
the earth, but visionary, earth luminous with sight:

49

it will be nearly half dark: contemplation dwells on
one thing at a time: it will have lows and highs,
basins and high countries, peaks and abysses, naked

seabottoms and naked summits: it will have interior
circulations, crusts in slow flotation: the wind
will blow through it and rock will confront it: it

will be oriented to polar transactions: nothing will
be left out, nothing, not a thing, and yet it will be
whole: there will be islands, island chains, bays,

50

peninsulas, bottom spreads, inland seas, and mind will
have below its active surface several layers of
sedimentary history, though below that will be the

melts in high heat and heavy pressure, the mobility
underlying encrustation and phenomenological flux:
there is one mind and one earth: it was all there

before it was first discovered and nothing will have
been added when it is fully elaborated: and yet it is
completely unknown until made out: then the cosmos:

51

why does he write poems: it's the only way he can mean
what he says: you mean, say what he means: yes,
but it's harder for him to mean something than say

something: his sayings are facile, light-headed, and
discontinuous: he keeps saying in order to hope he will
say something he means: poems help him mean what he says:

poems connect the threads between the tuft of his head
and the true water: that's important to him, like roots
to a turf: without it, the separation would be awful:

52

poems deepen his attention till what he is thinking
catches the energy of a deep rhythm: then he becomes
essentially one: one in thought and motion: then, he

means: the recent forward brain is working with the
medulla oblongata: by the time I get to the end of this
all, I'll have to have found something to say to the

people: this scratching around in the private self has
to yield something beyond a private waste of time: I
have to say, here is my drop of glue, now, somebody,

53

hold the world together, or just yourself: I have to say,
here is a saying, binding: I must not when I get up on
the soapbox wash out: here, I will say, is my offering

to the people, these few words right at the center of my
experience of me and you: the complicated, elaborate weaving
of interconnection: I want to do well: I want people to say,

did you hear that, that sounded good: perhaps I will say,
the cosmos, as I understand it, wants you to have fun:
or I will say, your deepest error may be divine:

54

much have I studied, trashcanology, cheesespreadology,
laboratorydoorology, and become much enlightened and
dismayed: have, sad to some, come to care as much for

a fluted trashcan as a fluted Roman column: flutes are
flutes and the matter is a mere substance design takes
its shape in: take any subject, everything gathers up

around it: friend of mine is studying barbedwireology
and he finds you can marshal up much world and history
around the discipline: barbedwire limitations and

55

intellectual definitions produce about the same
securities and disasters: I think a lot about meter and
right away it becomes the mirror in which I see the face

of the times: oh, but the hierarchy of subjects persists,
sociology way above scabology, philosophy a sight beyond
toothbrushosophy: the aristocracy of learning is so much

will: I'd as soon know one thing as another, what's the
difference, it all fits and comes out the same: and I
can tell you, I'd rather see a tempest in a teapot

56

than Shakespeare plain: but Shakespeare was all right:
a nursemaid's lip meant as much to him as the king's eye:
but he never got it straight that in talking about the

actual king and the symbolical king he was merely
engaging a problem in rhetoric: well, I'm glad because
I can't reconcile the one with the many either—except

in the fuzzy land of radiant talk—and if Shakespeare grossly
surpassing me failed, I don't have to worry about surpassing
others, my place comfortable in the lowerarchy:

57

work's never done: the difficult work of dying
remains, remains, and remains: a brain lobe squdging
against the skull, a soggy kidney, a little vessel

smartly plugged: wrestling with one—or those—until
the far-feared quietus comes bulby, floating, glimmer-wobbling
to pop: so much more mechanical, physical than

spiritual-seeming grief: than survivors' nights filled
without touch or word, than any dignity true for a state
of being: I won't work today: love, be my leisure:

58

there is something dwelling in too correspondent for
haphazardry: I read Plotinus once, a little, and
saw my mind (increased): currents, polar fads,

flash back and forth through a center apparently staid:
we may just now be getting enough lead into time to note
that nothing at all is moving except into the halfways

of diversion: what if at the core the final eye's
design's fixed, the vision beaming locked, we the motes
crossing about, breaking into and dropping out

59

of light: what if we're not seeking the light at all,
the transfixion (stare to stare in a bereft learning)
but worrying the corners of our confined, held

suasions for the exit we could, from the starved light,
choose: why has the dark taken so much if darkness is
not the satisfaction: and how have we found the will

to thrive through the light from sway to sway: O
Plotinus (Emerson, even) I'm just as scared as comforted
by the continuity, one sun spelling in our sun-made heads:

60

I exist by just so much as I am will-lessly borne
along: I am as given up as the boat-sloped maple leaf
on fast water: not a thing remains, not a motion's

curl, of any desire, and none of the things I desired
and gathered are with me: I deserve nothing, not
a glimpse into this world overbearingly rich, this

hungry, hardly-visionable air: just as empty as I am
is the just emptiness, not a leaf between here and
extinction I have not spent the night in luminous

61

supplication with: by just so much as a tide flows in
and lifts me floating, by just so much I can never
grin the deathgrin at the silver abundance until I must:

where I never came to self, repletion's an abundant
wind (I'm picking out the grains, gritty, between me
and that abundance): considerable as any least

burdockflower, I'm alive to the stalk tip: anything
cries salvation big as capturing a waterfall: by just
so much as I have given up, I am sustained till finally

62

the boat bumps solid, sucks the surface tit, and, bloated, drowns:
today's the first of the year, icicle, cloud, root
in a slow procedure, every house re-roofed with snow:

the biggest numbers represent the finest differences:
plus or minus two parts of variation in a trillion, as
in narrowing down on the inconstant readings of a

fundamental constant—the mass of the electron, the
speed of light, or the hyperfine splitting in hydrogen
proton precessions: nature seems firm with casual

63

certainties (one could say a steel spike is a foot
long) but pressed for certainty breaks out
in bafflings of variability, a thousand close

measurings of the spike averaged out and a thousand
efforts to average out the variables in the instruments
of measure or in the measuring environment

(room temperature, humidity, the probable frequency
the door to the room is opened): recalcitrance is built
in perfectly, variations thereon perceived as possibility:

64

oh, I'm going to walk right out onto th'elision fields,
eat up gloria in the morning and have it out with her
in the evening: I'm going to postpone reality (but for

cheeseburgers) and focus yearning, doubly focus it,
bring into view three-dimensional hopes and hokum:
dying here sour with flesh and sweat—the disposition

of nature's bounty, a bounteous abandonment to sludge,
desireless, breathless: otherwise, otherwise to the limit!
if all must come down, make a high possibility for the

65

dependable work, space out an extreme differential,
an illusion for the future: the poet entangles: the
critic untangles: the poet, baited by illusion, figures

that massive tangling will give locus to core-tangles
and core-tangles to *the* core-tangle that will
fix reality in staid complication, at that central

core's center the primordial egg of truth: ah, what an
illusion: from the undifferentiated core-serum the mind
turns back to the definition of its tangles for rescue

66

and then back to the core for clarification, only to
hesitate in quandary's puzzlement: carefully, the critic
unwinds thread from thread, making out the energy and

translating it into ratiocination: but the untangling
done, all the untangling done, nothing remains but the
dumb end of the last thread and the opus of statement

that replaces it: illusion! illusion! there are not
two somethings but two nothings: one nothing surrounds,
extends beyond, the fullest entanglement, and the other

67

nothing is an infinitesimal dot of void at the center of
the primordial egg: inside calls to outside: in between
is the choice, an impoverishment that does away even with

the egg, or an abundance of entanglement very much like
the world but also nothing: for myself, I would rather
wear beads than have no neck at all: the void is the

birthplace of finches, gyrfalcons, juncos (a specialty),
snowy egrets, woodcocks, hummingbirds, crows, jays,
wood ducks, warblers, titmice, and the end of everything:

68

I dreamed Edna St. Vincent Millay's female companion
had just arrived on the beach of Europe and was reciting
a moving poem about why had they come back when their old

friends had resettled or were lying in the sod: it was
a very sad poem and the lady was sad and wrinkled:
I woke up just before crying myself, impressed with

the power of the poetry and life's risky changes:
the morning was cloudless, rosy with atmosphere, the sun
already brightened to appear suddenly over the sudden ridge:

69

a little philosophy never hurt anybody: or else, little
philosophy hurts everybody: takes a lot of philosophy to
make a little philosopher: the bubble swells and bursts,

the leavings cherishable, as being of themselves, not
devoted to an organ of use but, as with balloons, dumbly
elastic, shrunk wrinkled, and, often, highly colorful:

constituting an encounter of thing to thing: the bubble
bursts and then one participates in the universal energy
of biting an apple, having a tooth filled, turning a

70

corner (the friction and earth-displacement of that) so
that the universe seems available in the
gravity of a ladybug tipped down a blade of grass:

there's a difference between division and differentiation:
from the primal energy, much has split away into identity—
toothpicks, yew berries, jungle gyms, pole beans (the

thoughtful differentiations into bell pepper and basil)—
but a little time undercuts these matters into shape (soon
they will be shapelessly available again) so that division

7 1

is, at most, temporal—(mind & body) ha! (mind & nature) ha!
(reality & appearance) ha! (dream & fact) ha!—no, no, this
is not an expression of division, of taxonomy, dogma, bouncy

triadic motion, structure, solidification, type, but of
identity differentiation: one of the strongest thrusts,
you might say, is to perish away from unity the fully

discrete, expressed, captured hollybush—the lust to
individuation we've heard so much about: let me, the cry
is, stand like the drop cast back from the breaking

7 2

crest apart and regard the other satisfactory expressions
so there may be action, interaction, contrariety, and sum:
but the rise into differentiation is exactly equal

to the fall, a just compact not too friendly to the
appetite ravingly incomplete, or something, the deflections
into limbo: routes go awry but everything anyhow gets

safely, if reluctantly, back into circulation, the
least differentiae nearest the continuum: it's true the
splits sometimes look perfect, the divisions ghastly, severe

7 3

alienation an agreeing merely with temporality: but actually
while the leaf may not answer one's questions, it waves, a
nice language, expressive and complete: and if the ladybug,

traveling across the droppy peaks of grass, seems not my friend,
then I have not understood hanging to cool in shade; or
legs nimbly feeling for grass-hair; or any other

sight-loud talk: if I pick a leaf, it wilts: if I cap a
spring, it swells: if I crush a grass-spear, it stains:
if the quince crowds the hollyhock, the hollyhock

74

bends away, suffering subtle losses of rectitude:
what am I to say: my brotherhood's immense, and if the gods
have vanished that were never here I do not miss them:

some universe comes here to my yard every day or so and bursts
into a fly standing, with six little dents, on water: sometimes
when I'm shaving, a real small fly, screen-penetrating, gets

stuck in a bowl-drop of water: but he wiggles and would be all
right if something could be done with the whole him, floating:
but when I touch a tissue to the drop of water, tension pulls him

75

down, crushing him limp, so he never gets up, no matter how
dry: a killing rescue: some things will not work: one day
I poured brine and salt-ice from the icecream freezer onto

a strip of ground near the hedge: earthworms walloped up
rampant and thrashing and then went puffy-limp and
white: I have killed I can't tell how many thousand priceless

moths and flies (even goldfinches and bright-streaked warblers)
sucked up by the grill or radiator grid: all of these lives
had been acting in accordance with given principles, identical

76

to my own: nothing's changed, with all the divisions
and terrors: the physical drowns and buoys, divides and comes
together: the bird's song-air's in my range, comes on my air:

I wrote the foregoing passage in July last year, which accounts
for the change of weather and some summery tone: and a
slightly longer line: winter is different, shortening:

if you believe in equivocation as a way then you
must also believe in univocation because that is one
of the possibilities of equivocation: and if you

77

believe all is fire why then everything is, including
the stones' dull music, solid, slow, and
cold: and the weatherless moon less is nevertheless

singing blips of meteoric bits, the flash
smirching to glistening moon-tears of solar effusions,
the wind, the solar wind, that pours out coronal lacings

into a great space: and then the mud by the swamp
ponds with cloud trails of crawdads scurrying is working
with little cellular thrivings: and the cool fire of

78

ferns climbing tree-footings from the deep freshets:
allow, allow for the cryogenic event even, low down
nearly where the atoms give up relation and drift in slow

falls, incredible, spaceless beads: that is an extreme
form of burning, say, but of the fire: I can't
help thinking that what we have is right enough, the

core of the galaxy, for example, a high condition,
ample, but here, though, on the surface at least,
toads, picnic tables, morning glories, firs afire:

79

the world seems to me a show closed down, a circus
left standing: the ropes slack, the loose tent
bellies and whomps in the wind like a scared gigantic

jellyfish: some stragglers are around but they are
turned inward on their purposelessness: they make up
directions that go nowhere: they turn missing corners:

the clown's paint has worn off: his rags have become
rags: his half-bald wig has become his head, his falls
have become his tricks: he now clowns to the universe:

80

now meter is interesting: the prospects are before
us: I feel the need for a realistic approach: we were
promised for today nine hours and six minutes of

daylight: we were promised no sunlight and received
none: but can you imagine forty degrees: we have it:
the ground is practically asplatter with eavesdropping:

there are pools under the floating mush: they are not
clearly of a depth: one must know the terrain well or
fill his boots: the garage, the cold garage, and the

81

porch still have six inches of snow but the house across
the way whose second floor is all under a slanting roof
is snow-free: the woods, unhung completely,

have resumed an old darkness, whereas yesterday they were
still irradiated with snowholdings: the sun,
invisible before, has set into another invisibility and

the consequences are darkening here through the clouds:
oh this little time-drenched world! how it jiggles with
flickering! light as history, as relic, light two

82

billion years old, moves its ancient telling through
the universe and deposits right here on my grass on a
clear night dim sediment of sizable duration: that

light can be so old and far-traveled, like flint, no
prayerstone that constant, the permanent telling of
that quickness: lucky that only by the equalizing instant

anything survives, lucky for us, who can thereby kiss
out time to a full reduction and know everything ravished,
burnt out in a lid's quickness: the total second:

83

sir, I told him, you have so many tones I can't tell
which one's prevailing: the dominant from the
predominant: you have so many, they come in chords,

tonic, subdominant, diminished: I can't tell the
significant significances from the insignificant
significances: won't you, I implored, thin out your

registration or, at least, give discernible direction
to your componency: it would take a battery of tonometers
just to find out about where you're at: in the

84

contextual sense: have something to say: say it:
need you spray sense and be trusted only in the spray's
shape: such enlargements of limitation often

fail into disorientation at the center: boo boo pee
doo: plot a course, Mr. Sulu: let's split: poetic
action mirrors human action: what preserves the

absurdist through the enactment of absurdity, what but
the feathery need to touch ideal absurdity: the
ideal's an imperishable validity: the illumination

85

identity takes thrust toward: it is the proposition
how we are to live our lives: the ideal hero and the
ideal anti-hero have ideality in common: heroes may

change ways, clothes, directions, moods, but all bear
the pressure of ideality: James, the train robber,
sublime: Appleseed, the life of service, yes:

the vacuum cleaner salesman can, in our time, hardly
give the imagination suction, gather dust into any
credible bag: rail splitter, spike driver, done, gone:

86

the sum of everything's nothing: very nice: that
turns the world back in on itself: such as right
when you possess everything, you'd give everything

up for a sickle pear: I hope my philosophy will turn
out all right and turn out to be a philosophy so as
to free people (any who are trapped, as I have been)

from seeking any image in the absolute or seeking
any absolute whatsoever except nothingness:
nothingness, far from being failure's puzzlement,

87

is really the point of lovely liberation, when
gloriously every object in and on earth becomes just
itself, total and marvelous in its exact scope,

able to exist without compromise out to the precise
skin-limit of itself: it allows freedom to fall
back from the thrust to the absolute into the world

so manifold with things and beings: the hollyhock,
what a marvel, complete in itself: the bee,
how particular, how nothingness lets him buzz

88

around: carless in Gaza, with a rocker arm on a valve
snapped, I to the gas station made it this morning,
left car, and by taxi so-forthed with son and wife

to University, son and wife going on beyond me to
nursery school: lunch hour nearing, I decided to
hitchhike home and did, first with a lady and baby

daughter all in a foreign small car, then with two
toughlooking guys from Virginia, leaned front seat
forward and let me in the back: we talked about

89

the snow, local squalls filling the air even though
the sun was shining: the driver said he had to get
back to Pennsylvania this afternoon: I asked if he had

snowtires and he said, No, and said he'd heard he could
get picked up if he got stuck without snowtires:
whereupon, apprehensively bound to be cheerful and useful,

I said when it's so cold like today the roads
stay dry even with the snow because the cars blow the
snow away as if it were feathers and that probably

90

he wouldn't have any trouble: just then a dog glanced
out onto the road, the driver, pushing back in his
seat, soaked on the brakes, and the car slid hardly at

all, verifying, as if by a universal complicity, my
faith's predictions: well, then, as we neared the
Corners, things seemed with me a little brighter, so

I said, that stop sign ahead would be perfect for me:
he would have to stop anyway, and I would know
immediately, if the other guy didn't open the door, that

91

I was about to be robbed, killed, or bent out of my will
which seemed about the worst thing: all went well,
ruining the story: I got out, saying thankyous and

wishingwells and walked about the mile down Hanshaw
home: just turning the curve in sight of home, I saw,
as in a perfect vision, my wife and son pulling up into

the driveway, driven back from nursery school in someone's
luminous stationwagon: I felt relieved: I said, ah, the
broken and divergent lines of morning are coalescing:

92

Wilde in some ways *contra naturam* really was: he loved
Art and set it against Nature, possibly because Art is
overwhelmed by Nature and he identified with being

overwhelmed: somewhat *contra mundum*, too: since
social nature had a majority against him: well, he did
rather well, a sort of terrier of the mind: he barked,

if mostly in the regions where opposites are clear, not
reconciled: I admire that: why think nature good if it's
against you: if it's against you, then it's hard to

93

approve even what produced you: not to approve what
produced you, though, bumfuzzles, since it's a kind
of suicidal vindication to hate nature in order to

love the self: how twisty things are: nature ought to
bear the blame, then, for fumbling, or society
learn to approve nature even when it fumbles, as being

also nature: well, I don't know what to hope in that
way, since society is also *contra naturam*, a device, a
convention: but if so how could Wilde come to love

94

convention so, I mean, convention as artifice, not the
conventional: Wilde, Art, Society, Convention—and then
convention damned him: that shuts off most of the roads

and suggests not detours but deadends: when a lioness
whelps a defective cub, she whomps it against the
ground till it's dead: well, I think we ought to put

ourselves above the beasts and take care to be respectful
where persons move: provided all persons move with
respect: we should exhaust all our virtues, first:

95

though it's gooseegg zero, morning sunlight hits the
strip of woods broadside and a squirrel is sitting out
pretty still on a limb taking in the direct radiation:

enormous jungle-like fronds of ice (and other configurations
like species) have run across possessing the outer windows
but, now, the sun up, thaw like a fungus is making dark

melts in the foliage: the sun's arc rises a little
daily into the world, marking a slightly longer
journey along the ridge between rising and setting:

96

yesterday afternoon, right after I had written about
the adventures of the morning, the gas station called and
said my car was ready: I had been thinking how many

days, not how many hours, it would take: so John, that's
his name up at Ned's Corners Station, drove the car on
down here to 606, less than a mile, and I made out a

check for him ($19.39), dropped him back at the station,
and took off for the University, free and mobilized again!
the total parts came to $7.79, 1 push rod ($1.25), 1

97

rocker arm ($1.35), 1 rocker retainer ($0.50), 1 set 2
gaskets @ $2.10 ($4.20), and 1 roll electrical tape ($0.49):
the total labor was $10.50: r & r (remove and repair?)

l. (left?) valve cover, r & r both valve covers, replace
rocker arm, push rod, & retainer on #4 cyl intake valve:
all in all I thought I got off easy: one thing interesting

is that Ned's Corners Station is at 909 Hanshaw Road
and I'm 606 Hanshaw Road: that's configuration:
today is, as I said, bright and cold: but 9 hrs 12 min.:

98

everyday (somedays, twice) I remember who I am and I
metamorphose away through several distracting transformations
till I get myself out in bidable shape on comfortable

ground, and then the shows, the transactions, carry
traces of such brilliant energy of invention that I am
half willing to admire my new self, thrust into its

lofty double helices, so winding: well, that's one way
to get out of the dumps, but they say it's wiser to
find the brilliants right in the dumps themselves: but on

99

the show side, there's not only the show itself, bodiless
if arresting, but the honest mechanisms that produced
the show: those mechanisms are earnest and work to

conserve their energy through transformations with a
greater efficiency than you can find anywhere in the
dumps: I mean, the quantity of structured mass you have

at the end is almost perfectly equal to that at the
beginning: on the dump, though, fire, efficient,
will achieve nothing but ash, heat, and smoke: excellent

100

change, but poor payload: or take rust, sluggish,
but it operates okay, not that you can do much with
ironic dust: the thing is to derive the *jus commune*

from the *jus singulare:* never must the *jus commune*
breeze through eradicating the *jus singulare:* the *jus
commune* must be merely a fall-out from happenstance:

that way it can find some curvature (if any) with the
actual: otherwise, the *jus commune* might become clear
to itself and propose imposition: never: never never:

101

I don't think I want to be buried here in these rocky
hills: once underground, how could I ever get my arms
free of the silk and steel, how could I ever with those

feet travel through the earth to my sweet home country
where all the flesh that bore me, back through grandfathers
and grandmothers, lies, and my little

brothers and my little sister I never saw, born before
me and dying small: and where will my living sisters
be put down, not here, and their children who might

102

visit me sometime to weep: but, a running weed,
I've come off up here and started a new offshoot
nucleus of a family and that sort of act perhaps should

be run into the ground: I mean, extended, preserved
into the ground: but this is phantasmagoria: death's
indifference will absorb living nostalgias and, anyway,

earth's a single mother and all who lie in her are brothers
and sisters: jungle cats and mudcats, sleek and slick:
the other night on Hee-Haw somebody said, "slick as

103

a mudcat's fin:" that's slick: poetry to the people,
not that they will ever acknowledge it: well, it's
night now and still fair, the moon full: the temperature

is dropping and the heater picking up: I put John's
tent together in the basement this afternoon: 8 rods
of fiberglass, connected with flexible tubes into 4

lengths, those then run through the sleeves, aluminum
sleeves adding support at the joints, and all brought
together at the top: a zipper door: his little house:

104

I looked up man in the dictionary and he was illustrated
and, as it turned out, chiefly muscle, a red fabric, and
bone, the whiteness men share: this creature, I

thought, has taken over, I know not whether because of
the freedom of the fingerbones or of the wagging, detachable
jaw, one about as gross and fine as the other: he

depends, ultimately, I thought again, on grass but, my,
what a transfiguration from the grass: he sees, his
vision air-clear: he tastes and feels: he thinks, ah:

105

he devours: he falls into necessities, or madnesses, only
his body can untangle: he carries in his lobed, zoned
skull earth's little supernova, the cerebral explosion,

somewhat in its stems and exfoliations like a mushroom
cloud: in him is ticking the californium 254 he's
detected in bombs and stars, whether still in its

first or some lesser half-life, unknown: but his little
explosion is growing up to equal celestial models: for
example, the other night the paper said two nearby

106

galaxies, hidden by our Milky Way, have been found, sight
having made other kinds of sight hunting, eating, loving
had no use for, some high conditions of burning: oh, yes,

we're *in* the explosions and we're going to see them out
and no other course could be half as interesting: falling
back can't help us now, returning to nature's lovely

subtle mechanisms: forward to the finish, of course, the
way it's always been or to a knowledge how to avoid the
finish: the possibility seen through to its perfect end:

107

the young are earnest, impatient: the older have learned
the alternatives, to be wrecked or reconciled: oh,
but it's not that easy: combinations and degrees make

life rough and rugged: yuck, yuck, the muck-sleet sings
pone the midnight windowpane, and the shattery wind
the shutters shudders: the confessor yanks up a belch

of privacy gone to seed: orangutans aren't groupy
as gorillas: cello alto solo pronto: if there is to be
no principle of inclusion, then, at least, there ought

108

to be a principle of exclusion, for to go with a maw at
the world as if to chew it up and spit
it out again as one's own is to trifle with terrible

affairs: I think I will leave out China, the perturbations
and continuities, transmutations and permutations of
Chinese civilization because, since that is so much,

giving it up's an immediate and cordial act of abasement,
betokening readiness to leave the world alone as
currently constituted (but, of course, how could words

109

do otherwise!): but I'm willing also to leave out most,
if not all, of the Amazon basin (all those trees, what
a whack), millions of islands I've never heard of and

some big ones I have, all ocean bottoms, all very high
places (whose spirituality blurs me), nearly all clouds
(which come and go lots before they pass through here), and,

if the population of the earth is four billion people,
then nearly four billion people: am I safe yet: of
course not: principles of exclusion become inclusive, etc.:

110

hiatuses, non-sequiturs, and indiligences later (nine hours
and forty-three minutes daylight) federal reorganizations
and revenue-sharings, advancings on extremely heavy

volume, what is everything about or anything for:
procedure's the only procedure: if things don't add
up, they must interest at every moment: a

difficulty: yesterday, severe, high-altitude winds
took our lower atmospheres in tow, making highly-compressed
bottom stirs, thunder at noon, one flash and blam,

111

and an even mixture of snow, rain, and sleet: zero
visibility was visible as near waves and white streams:
today is iron-fist windy and nudging zero: outside the

pheasant have lost all fear: they hunker down by the
picket fence, inattentive as the enemyless, or knowing
the enemy, too, must bear the cold: the ground is

assuming the curvatures of wind, flat-open places skinned
clean of snow, interruptions by fall-out being built up
to, mounds with sharp precipices, sometimes a mound

112

breaking loose into strings of fast snow: I am unnerved
by openness and pure prose: the blue spruce is like
sprinkled with white crowsfeet, the inner intensive stems

branching, holding snow the needles can't: and into the
huge, round yew bush starlings light and go two-thirds
under: they peck the frit of snow the wind leaves

and drink: I'm reading Xenophon's *Oeconomicus* "with
considerable pleasure and enlightenment" and with
appreciation that saying so fills this stanza nicely.

DATE DUE